Col

ISA.
40:31

Hebrews 12:1
12:12-13
2 TIM 4:7

LIVE LOVE

BECOMING LIKE CHRIST IN THOUGHT, SPEECH, AND ACTION

VAN BRADEEN

First Printing: 2017

ISBN-978-1-548999414

Cover design by Amani Hanson (Becoming Studios, noboxez@yahoo.com).

Editing, text design and typesetting by Jim Bryson (JamesLBryson@gmail.com).

Proofreading by Emilyanne Zornes (pcome.proofandcopy@gmail.com)

Endorsements

The first thing I look for in a book is to see if the author's words are supported with scripture, as it is the word of God that transforms lives. *Live Love* is full of scripture and every chapter brings a challenge to the reader. In addition, it's not just theory but has been lived out by the author. Thanks, Pastor Van, for this helpful, well-written discipleship tool.

Pastor Dick Iverson
Founder—City Bible Church, Portland, OR
Founder—Minister Fellowship International
Founder—Portland Bible College
Author of several books thru City Christian Publishing

*****

This is a wonderfully practical book authored by a man who understands his mission in life. Van Bradeen's grace gift and clarity in God's word 'fix' the great commission into a way of life. Here is valuable material that benefits small groups, assimilation, and a healthy culture for the local church. As you read, we learn to love the journey of discipleship and the closeness with Christ and people it brings. More than mere talk, you'll find yourself empowered to live out our love, which is the goal of our faith. I found it packed full of greatly needed tools for every believer! Here's hoping we read it and lead it.

Lon Stokes
Staff Pastor—Life Church, Walla Walla, WA.

Live Love is a book forged in the furnace of a life yielded to the God who makes all things new. Therefore, if anyone is in Christ, he is a new creation; old things have passed away; behold, all things have become new (2 Corinthians 5:17 (NKJV)).

Salvation transforms the heart, but discipleship brings our life into conformity with the cry of that new heart. Van has written a book with just the right mixture of biblical truth and practical life experience to help us on that journey to live and love like Jesus. This is more than just another book on discipleship; this is a grateful man's life passion written for those he learned to love.

Pastor Bob Johnson
Pastor—New City Church, Great Falls, MT
Director—Advance Pastors Network
Regional Director—Ministers Fellowship International

*****

I don't believe I've met another pastor/leader that has as much of a laser focus on discipling people as Van Bradeen. *Live Love* is right from the heart of a leader and is valuable for personal devotions, small groups or larger gatherings. *Live Love* is filled with both pointed and personal examples to follow in your journey, you will be changed!

Jeff Ecklund
Lead Pastor—House of The Lord in Oldtown, ID
Author—*Wholehearted*

*****

I have known Van for over 10 years and his heart has always been to see people saved and become disciples of Jesus. He does not pull any punches as he walks us through what is looks like to *Live Love* as Jesus did. The conviction of the Holy Spirit will be your closest companion as Van continually points to scriptures that highlight our need for transformation in our life. The use of teaching, application, and the response portion at the end of each chapter challenges every reader, from newly saved to decades in the faith, to allow the Holy Spirit to transform the areas in our lives that don't look like Jesus.

Ben Meckel
Generation Pastor—City Harvest Church, Vancouver, WA
(Ben's passion is to see people operate in their gifts to extend the kingdom of God.)

*****

God has shown us immeasurable mercy and grace, and so became the ultimate example of love that we should desire to lavish on one another. This book gives us insights directly from Scripture, to increase our passion and heartbeat to both reach out to the lost and serve one another with deep love. Pastor Van shares with us, through *Live Love*, the tools every Christian needs in order to operate in fully, living as Christ did.

Kathy Marcolin
Victory Faith Church, Spokane, WA
(Kathy's passion is to minister to women so they can walk in the freedom that Christ offers.)

*****

This book is an easy to understand journey through the words of God that help build relationship and discipleship. Van's story shared through the process helps provide entertainment and context to the lessons being learned. I highly recommend letting *Live Love* lead you on a journey to be more like Jesus.

Bobby Carmody
Community Pastor—Heart of the City Church.

Dedication

First to Jesus who pursued me, showed me His love, kindness and mercy, and spoke to me through His word even as I rejected Him. His Holy Spirit convicted me of sin for the first two years of college as He gently surrounded me with His love. I strongly believe I would be in hell now without Jesus' saving grace and pursuit.

Second, to my wife of 28 years, Lori, who married this zealous convert to Christ knowing he had a long way to go, but she loved him anyway. Yeah, I had a lot to learn and we learned it together. Through thick and thin, love and grace, three great kids, and a thriving ministry, we've walked this road hand in hand…in hand.

Finally, to Pastor Bob and Sue MacGregor of City Harvest Church. Pastor Bob walked with me for 12 years. I was a raw mountain man from an Indian Reservation who needed a lot of help in pastoring people. Pastor Bob understood my passion to shepherd and personally taught me the elements presented here. He truly lives love.

Contents

K

L

Foreword

It is interesting that in today's church, so many people are looking for a spirituality that is either found in subjective experiences with quick fixes or in the pursuit of deeper meaning to scripture, discovering things no one has seen before. Yet Jesus of Nazareth laid out the true essence of spirituality in His answer to a lawyer seeking the greatest commandment. He simply said, *"'Love the Lord your God with all your heart and with all your soul and with all your mind.' This is the first and greatest commandment. And the second is like it: 'Love your neighbor as yourself.' All the Law and the Prophets hang on these two commandments."* (Matthew 22:37-40).

Paraphrased, Jesus is telling us: "Love God with every emotion, passion, and mental focus that is in us and love people as much as we love and care for ourselves." Jesus said that everything that the Old Testament had taught and revealed up to His time was about those two things—loving God and loving people.

That's it? No deep revelation? No pilgrimage to a some "Mecca" where God hangs out? No, it is simply about pursuing God to know and love God radically, and loving people with the same intensity as we love ourselves.

There are two great challenges to Jesus' simple commandments. One is that something simple isn't necessarily easy. This is what President Ronald Reagan said about America's problems: The answers are simple but not easy. The same is true with what Jesus taught. His teachings are simple but not easy. It is not easy to love people who frustrate you, hurt you, demand things from you, criticize you, and inconvenience you in daily life experiences. We would rather withdraw, avoid, isolate, or try something new. We romanticize that somewhere out there is a new spouse, friend, church, job, or region that will be easier to love. So we forsake our moral responsibility to love, instead seeking our fantasy somewhere else, never learning and never growing.

Then there is the alternative of forgetting people altogether, withdrawing into a cocoon of seclusion where we and Jesus can be alone as He reveals to us deeper and deeper insights through a spirituality void of relational conflict, moral responsibility, and mutual submission. God plus us is all we need. The problem with this position is that Jesus taught that true spirituality involves people, those we must serve, love, forgive, learn from, submit to, suffer with, put-up with, and yes...forgive. This second challenge involves a lot of painful growth.

We can see why it is so easy for us to step around human need, join a monastery, set boundaries that divorce ourselves completely from any suffering, and dive into the latest devotional book telling us of God's promises we can claim and how much He loves us. Somehow, we deceive ourselves that we can become like Jesus by avoiding people. It is like someone who wants to look like a body builder without ever hitting the gym.

True spiritual growth will not allow us to take such a route. To love people and to dwell with them in community as family requires something from us that is easier said than done—we must die to ourselves so we can live for others. The message of the cross confronts us when reflecting upon all Christ did for us, calling on us to do the same for others. A gospel-focused follower of Christ understands the cross and makes it the center of their life, not only by embracing and appreciating what Christ did for us but by giving himself or herself to others in the same manner. Any teaching, theological study, or new revelation is incomplete and incompatible with the Bible if it does not include Jesus' mandate to *"love your neighbor as yourself"* (Mark 12:31) by living it out in Christian community.

Of course, this involves the church, that group of imperfect people that Jesus Christ calls to live a different lifestyle and connect with one another as His new temple; the church that He said He would build; the church that involves carnal, human people who experience relational conflict and bring out the worst hostilities in one another; the church flawed and full of failures. This is what Jesus is building, yet in all her imperfections, He has purposed to use her to make you and me like Him. Yes, Jesus is a tough trainer, but if we can endure the rigor of living in community with one another, we just might become the people He has called us to be. We just might begin to reflect Jesus to the world.

I have known Van and Lori Bradeen for twenty years. During this time, I have been their pastor, mentor, and friend. I have watched them live out the "one another" mandate of the New Testament. They were excellent servants on my pastoral team and were loved by those they touched. They are known as people who are motivated for others. Loyal, honest, and humble, they have pursued the true meaning of living in community as they have chased their dreams and destiny. The church they pastor, Living Stone Church in Spokane, Washington, is a reflection of the reality of their conviction to live out the "one another" mandate of the Bible.

As you study the truths laid out in Pastor Van Bradeen's book, *Live Love*, you will be challenged to live out the simple but not-so-easy life of living for others. You will be confronted with the need to embrace the cross and die to self. However, you will find on the other side of obedience to the principles of this book, the abundant life that Jesus Christ promised He would give us and the great key to becoming like Christ. Do not fear this route and take the easy way, because life is at the end of this narrow but beautiful way that He wants us to walk.

Bob MacGregor

Lead Pastor, City Harvest Church

1

Beginning the Transformation

Be transformed...

Romans 12:2

In the spring of 1987, as I sat in my dorm room at Eastern Washington University (EWU), the Spirit of God came upon me in a way I will never forget.

I was on top of the world, playing college football and living the dream, but my worldly dreams crashed around me as Jesus walked through my door. This God experience was intensely real—my body was consumed with a wave of supernatural power. As I felt His presence, Jesus showed me heaven and hell and the choice I had to make. Although I didn't fully realize it at the time, I was on a collision course for an eternity in hell without Him. I repented of my sins and gave my life to Christ, then spent the next three hours weeping on the floor as Jesus showed me what it meant to follow Him and love people. From that moment on, everything in my life, including football, took a back seat to Jesus and the love He gave me for people's souls.

Whenever I think back on that day, God's love for people wells up within me. Thirty years ago, Jesus showed me His desire that people would walk out His love, living like Him in thought, speech, and action. Jesus lived a perfect life, demonstrating how to love people, leading us in the way we are to follow.

My heart is to see Christians walk in a deep, meaningful relationship with God and others. This can only be accomplished as we purposely seek Him with all our hearts, crucifying our flesh as we apply the Word of God to every area of our lives.

In sharing this message, I hope to challenge you to the very core of your being. In the process, we will learn how to live out key elements of God's transformative power: repentance, obedience, forgiveness, reconciliation, transformation, self-evaluation, crucifying the flesh, and the fear of the Lord

Write them out

Our goal is to *Live Love*.

LIVE LOVE

What does it mean to live love? It starts with pursuing Jesus, experiencing His great love and compassion, and walking in freedom. It means growing to love people, desiring that they follow Jesus with all their hearts. It means developing a single eye to follow God's will just as Jesus did. It means obeying the word of God, causing our selfish thoughts and desires to fall by the wayside. Finally, it means weeping for lost souls just as Jesus does.

I want to guide you into a deeper, passionate, and more intimate relationship with Jesus, to a place where His thoughts, speech, and actions become a part of you, supplanting your flesh—the sin nature.

The key to intimacy with God is our pursuit of Him. God has done all the work we will ever need. He sent His Son Jesus Christ to die in our place. When Jesus rose from the dead, He conquered death itself. Finally, in God's great love and compassion, He poured out His Spirit so we can walk in the power and love of Jesus. God has done His part; we now have to pursue Him with all of our heart.

ONE ANOTHER

God wants us to learn to love *Him* more so that we can love *people* more. The Apostle Paul shared God's heart, and he knew that if he could get believers to love deeper, the church would become stronger. So, he taught the church relational goals in the form of "one-another" phrases.

Let's look at each one of these.

- Members of one another.

  For as in one body we have many members, and the members do not all have the same function, so we, though many, are one body in Christ, and individually members one of another.

  Romans 12:4-5 (NASB)

- Building up one another.

  Therefore encourage one another and build each other up, just as in fact you are doing.

  1 Thessalonians 5:11

- Loving one another.

  Above all, love each other deeply, because love covers over a multitude of sins. Offer hospitality to one another without grumbling.

  1 Peter 4:8-9

- Pursue one another's good and do not repay evil for evil.

Live Love

So I strive always to keep my conscience clear before God and man.

Acts 24:16

- Care for and encourage one another and help the weak.

Hold them in the highest regard in love because of their work. Live in peace with each other. And we urge you, brothers and sisters, warn those who are idle and disruptive, encourage the disheartened, help the weak, be patient with everyone.

1 Thessalonians 5:13-14

- Help bear the burdens of one another.

Carry each other's burdens, and in this way you will fulfill the law of Christ.

Galatians 6:2

- Be kind and compassionate to one another.

Be kind and compassionate to one another, forgiving each other, just as in Christ God forgave you.

Ephesians 4:32

- Consider others more significant than yourself.

Do nothing out of selfish ambition or vain conceit. Rather, in humility value others above yourselves, 4 not looking to your own interests but each of you to the interests of the others.

Philippians 2:3-4

- Forgive one another and live in harmony with others.

Bear with each other and forgive one another if any

Be balanced

4

of you has a grievance against someone. Forgive as the Lord forgave you.

Colossians 3:13

Live in harmony with one another. Do not be proud, but be willing to associate with people of low position. Do not be conceited.

Romans 12:16

- The ultimate proof of Living Love is obeying Jesus.

  We know that we have come to know him if we keep his commands.

1 John 2:3

Our study will follow these "one-another" goals, one per chapter. We will learn to take God's word and apply it to our lives, cutting away our sinful tendencies, learning to forgive and releasing the bitterness that blocks relationship with Jesus and others. God's heart is for us to be free of anything that hinders us from loving others. This is true freedom as accomplished through God's grace, not through our own religious strength! Trying to gain God's approval through our works is legalism. Jesus bridged the only road to the Father in heaven. He is so passionate about living with us that He surrendered His life on the cross that we might have eternal life. He then ascended on high, pouring out His Spirit that we might be consumed with His righteousness, peace, and joy. We are to walk in His strength and help others do the same.

As we pursue Jesus and His words, we become like Him, keeping His commands from the sincere desires of our hearts.

Whoever says, "I know Him," but does not do what He commands is a liar, and the truth is not in that person. But if anyone obeys His word, love for God is truly made complete in them. This is how we know we are in Him.

1 John 2:4-5

You, my brothers and sisters, were called to be free. But do not use your freedom to indulge the flesh; rather, serve one another humbly in love. For the entire law is fulfilled in keeping this one command: "Love your neighbor as yourself." If you bite and devour each other, watch out or you will be destroyed by each other.

Galatians 5:13-15

BECOMING MORE LIKE CHRIST

As we pursue this study, we will learn to apply God's perfect and penetrating word to every area of our lives, breaking the chains of sin in all its incarnations: lust, jealousy, envy, selfishness, bitterness, unforgiveness, anxiety, depression, insecurity, pride, and every fleshly desire.

As we are filled with the word of God through the Holy Spirit, we will understand that the way to live love is not to show God that we can reach Him in our strength alone, but to agree with God that His word is our change agent. As we look into God's word, we evaluate our true condition through His eyes. If any part of our being (body, soul, spirit) is not in alignment with God's word, we repent of our sin, crucify our flesh, and ask God for more of His perfect grace, love, and strength to be imparted into our life.

The book of Hebrews shows us that God's perfect word penetrates our beings, even to the intentions of our thoughts, so we can be transformed to be like Jesus.

> *¹² For the word of God is alive and active. Sharper than any double-edged sword, it penetrates even to dividing soul and spirit, joints and marrow; it judges the thoughts and attitudes of the heart. ¹³ Nothing in all creation is hidden from God's sight. Everything is uncovered and laid bare before the eyes of him to whom we must give account.*

Hebrews 4:12-13

Applying God's word to our lives keeps us in God's will by aligning our hearts with His heart. God's instructions to Israel in Deuteronomy 17:14-20, regarding the kings of Israel, shows us the importance of God's word and how it works in our lives.

> *¹⁴When you enter the land the LORD your God is giving you and have taken possession of it and settled in it, and you say, "Let us set a king over us like all the nations around us," ¹⁵ be sure to appoint over you a king the LORD your God chooses. He must be from among your fellow Israelites. Do not place a foreigner over you, one who is not an Israelite. ¹⁶ The king, moreover, must not acquire great numbers of horses for himself or make the people return to Egypt to get more of them, for the LORD has told you, "You are not to go back that way again." ¹⁷ He must not take many wives, or his heart will be led astray. He must not accumulate large amounts of silver and gold.*
>
> *¹⁸ When he takes the throne of his kingdom, he is to write for himself on a scroll a copy of this law, taken*

from that of the Levitical priests. [19] It is to be with him, and he is to read it all the days of his life so that he may learn to revere the LORD his God and follow carefully all the words of this law and these decrees [20] and not consider himself better than his fellow Israelites and turn from the law to the right or to the left. Then he and his descendants will reign a long time over his kingdom in Israel.

Deuteronomy 17:14-20

Notice that a new King was required to personally rewrite the first five books of the Bible in front of the priestly leadership. This was to get the words deep in his heart, ensuring that he would fear and obey the Lord throughout his reign. As the king read God's word daily, it would keep him from exalting himself above his fellow countrymen. As long as the king walked out God's commands and made godly decisions for the country, God would bless Israel. If he didn't, the entire nation would suffer.

The same holds true for us today; we are to read God's word daily, allowing the Holy Spirit to conform us to His thoughts, speech, and actions, enabling us to live love.

God designed biblical repentance to heal, restore, and refresh us. And while the conviction leading to repentance isn't always comfortable, it should never be seen as a punishment from God. Rather, it is God reaching out in His perfect love, offering freedom to live a guiltless life. To have an intimate relationship with Jesus, we must allow Him to penetrate our hearts and minds.

APPLICATION

In the application section of each chapter, I will present scriptures detailing God's view on a subject. By understanding clearly what God is saying about something, we can evaluate our own positions and allow God to change us. This is the heart of Hebrews 4:12-13.

Here, for example, we will take the issue of sexual immorality in our culture, an issue affecting everyone—Christians and non-Christians alike.

SEX AND CULTURE

Some of the greatest sins in our culture involve sexual immorality—sexual activity outside of God's plan and purpose. The issues are so pervasive that many Christians have fallen into worldly opinions about sex. I know this from personal experience. I was engrossed in immorality when Jesus saved me. When I surrendered to Him, He began to gently change me, leading me to the scriptures that confronted every aspect of my life.

Here are some of the scriptures God used to change me. See how they apply to your life. This purpose is not just to understand sexual immorality, but to learn the process of comparing our opinions with God's and choosing that which is right. Our goal is to adjust our perspective to God's perfect word, being molded into the image of Christ.

> It is God's will that you should be sanctified: that you should avoid sexual immorality;
>
> 1 Thessalonians 4:3

> In a similar way, Sodom and Gomorrah and the surrounding towns gave themselves up to sexual immorality and perversion. They serve as an example of those who suffer the punishment of eternal fire.
>
> Jude 1:7

Live Love

Put to death, therefore, whatever belongs to your earthly nature: sexual immorality, impurity, lust, evil desires and greed, which is idolatry.

Colossians 3:5

But among you there must not be even a hint of sexual immorality, or of any kind of impurity, or of greed, because these are improper for God's holy people.

Ephesians 5:3

You say, "Food for the stomach and the stomach for food, and God will destroy them both." The body, however, is not meant for sexual immorality but for the Lord, and the Lord for the body.

1 Corinthians 6:13

But I tell you that anyone who looks at a woman lustfully has already committed adultery with her in his heart.

Matthew 5:28

Here is a lengthy passage from Romans on the subject. It is worth the read.

For although they knew God, they neither glorified him as God nor gave thanks to him, but their thinking became futile and their foolish hearts were darkened. [22] Although they claimed to be wise, they became fools [23] and exchanged the glory of the immortal God for images made to look like a mortal human being and birds and animals and reptiles.

[24] Therefore God gave them over in the sinful desires of their hearts to sexual impurity for the degrading

of their bodies with one another. ²⁵ They exchanged the truth about God for a lie, and worshiped and served created things rather than the Creator—who is forever praised. Amen.

²⁶ Because of this, God gave them over to shameful lusts. Even their women exchanged natural sexual relations for unnatural ones. ²⁷ In the same way the men also abandoned natural relations with women and were inflamed with lust for one another. Men committed shameful acts with other men, and received in themselves the due penalty for their error.

²⁸ Furthermore, just as they did not think it worthwhile to retain the knowledge of God, so God gave them over to a depraved mind, so that they do what ought not to be done. ²⁹ They have become filled with every kind of wickedness, evil, greed and depravity. They are full of envy, murder, strife, deceit and malice. They are gossips, ³⁰ slanderers, God-haters, insolent, arrogant and boastful; they invent ways of doing evil; they disobey their parents; ³¹ they have no understanding, no fidelity, no love, no mercy. ³² Although they know God's righteous decree that those who do such things deserve death, they not only continue to do these very things but also approve of those who practice them.

Romans 1:21-32

This is how I see the heart of this passage. When we disobey God—when we purposely sin in sexual immorality—we are telling God that what He created is wrong and that instead, we are going to do whatever we want to. As we fall into deeper sexual sin, we begin to feel the strong conviction of the Holy Spirit, yet we continue to sin. Thus, we continue to tell God that His way is wrong and our way is right. Finally, calamity strikes—we lose our health, our spouse, our freedom, or our ability to relate to others in a sexually healthy way. Unable to accept our own accountability, we blame God for our problems. We are not only diseased by the scourge of sin, we are also deceived—divorced from truth—and have no recourse but to repent or accept the penalty of our ways. *For the wages of sin is death, but the gift of God is eternal life in Christ Jesus our Lord* (Romans 6:23).

STRAIGHT AND NARROW

To live love means to obey every part of God's word and reject what the world says. Jesus told us in Matthew 7:13-14:

> *Enter through the narrow gate. For wide is the gate and broad is the road that leads to destruction, and many enter through it. But small is the gate and narrow the road that leads to life, and only a few find it.*

As God's word highlights our sin through comparison to His perfect way, we will find ourselves crying out to God as King David did.

> *Test me, LORD, and try me, examine my heart and my mind; for I have always been mindful of your unfailing love and have lived in reliance on your faithfulness.*
>
> Psalm 26:2-3

Crying out to the Lord is more than wailing into the heavens. It is a deliberate posturing of our being such that we can receive Jesus' redemptive work. The Holy Spirit is ready to search us, purge us, and restore us. Only we can allow Him, and only we can stop Him. God gave us all scripture so we can learn to obey Him by leaning on Him to restore our minds and heart to the mind of Christ.

As we compare our position to God's, there are a few things that we must solidify in our minds.

1. Obedience to God's word is the ultimate form of love.

2. God's word is perfect and we must come in alignment with it, not the other way around.

3. If our life is in opposition or contrast to what God's word says, it is we who must change. The Holy Spirit changes our hearts and minds to align with God.

4. We cannot negotiate with God on matters of sin. He is just, perfect, holy, without sin, full of love and compassion, and an all-consuming fire. In other words, He is God and we are not. We must conform to Him.

5. As scripture confronts our thoughts and actions, God will give us the grace to change. This is called sanctification.

6. God's grace is our ability to walk godly. Everything we do in our Christian life should be empowered by God's amazing grace.

7. The enemy of our soul will do everything possible to keep us from repenting of our sin and receiving God's grace.

SELF-EVALUATION OR GROUP DISCUSSION

- Rate yourself on a 1-5 scale (1=bad, 5=excellent) on your desire to completely obey God's word in all areas of your life.

- Based on the scriptures in this chapter, why do you think God is adamant about sexual purity?

- How does your current perspective on sexual morality align with God's word?

  o You can be honest. I have faced the same issues. After I got saved, I knew that sexual intercourse outside of marriage was wrong because the Spirit of God convicted me of that, but until I actually studied the scriptures, I still thought everything else was fine. In other words, my opinion and feelings didn't align with God's word until I allowed God's word to penetrate my heart as it says in Hebrews 4:12-13.

- To what extent is our culture out of alignment with God's intended purposes for sex?

- What are some destructive things that happen in our culture that result from a sexual "do what you want attitude"?

- What are the public health risks of having sex outside of marriage or with multiple partners?

- How do we lovingly help others obey God in all areas of life, especially when our culture teaches: "Do what you want"?

- How do we effectively confront people with their sexual sin, offering them the truth of God's word instead of cultural norms?

  o Hint: Galatians 6:1-2

- To what extent are we following Jesus' example regarding sex? According to the Bible, He ministered to many women who had sinful sex lives: multiple marriages, harlotry, and adultery. Yet His heart was always to bring them to wholeness. It was never to take advantage of them.

Here is the bottom line: If you want to be free from sexual sin, you must take the scriptures on sex and begin to read and pray through them daily until your thoughts become the thoughts of Jesus.

...But we have the mind of Christ.

1 Corinthians 2:16

The more your heart desires to obey God, the more the Holy Spirit will help you desire to obey—which leads to living love—becoming more like Christ in thought, speech, and action.

JOURNAL

One thing that helped change my life as I learned to walk with Jesus was to journal—writing down everything the Holy Spirit was telling me. This included scripture, things to repent of, or people with whom I needed to restore relationship. I'd write it all down and pray over it, seeking His grace. Often, Jesus would give me a scripture that spoke targeted truth into my life, helping me in times of need. There were times when Jesus had me rewrite entire books of the Bible, just as the kings of Israel did, so I could get His word deep into my spirit.

Most of us carry burdens from offenses, wounds, or lies about ourselves or God. The Holy Spirit wants to relieve us of our baggage. Take the time to write what the Holy Spirit is doing in your life, and allow His perfect work in your life.

The weapons we fight with are not the weapons of the world. On the contrary, they have divine power to demolish strongholds. We demolish arguments and every pretension that sets itself up against the knowledge of God, and we take captive every thought to make it obedient to Christ. And we will be

15

*ready to punish every act of disobedience, once your
obedience is complete.*

2 Corinthians 10:4-6

The more we prayerfully write out God's word, the more our
thoughts and actions will conform to His will, making us more like
Jesus and leading us to live love. On the other hand, if we ignore
His word, we will never change. As we are devoted to God's perfect
word, God will be devoted to changing us for good.

PRAYER

Each chapter will end with a simple prayer asking God to come
and give us more of His Spirit as He purges more of our sinful nature.

Father, in Jesus name, I come to You and ask for You to fill me
with more of Your Holy Spirit. I repent of any sin in my life that
keeps me in bondage of guilt and shame. I am asking You, Jesus, to
cleanse me and set me free. Holy Spirit, please consume me with
Your presence and help me walk in Your power and grace. Lord,
as I examine these scriptures in Chapter 1, I repent of all sexual
immorality. I repent of any inappropriate sexual interest I have
towards anyone. I want my life to line up with You, Jesus. I need
You to flood my life with Your holy conviction and grace. Jesus,
help me repent of anything in my life that is out of alignment with
Your word. Jesus, I want my heart and mind to be transformed by
Your word, so I take on *Your* heart and mind. Amen.

NOTES

<u>Live Love</u>

2

Members of One Another

And let us consider how we may spur one another on toward love and good deeds, not giving up meeting together, as some are in the habit of doing, but encouraging one another—and all the more as you see the Day approaching.

Hebrews 10:24-25

As a church leader for nearly 30 years, I have seen many people commit their lives to Jesus but never finish the race. By far the saddest experiences of being a pastor have been watching people come into the church and have a wonderful experience with the Holy Spirit, stay for a season, and then leave because they are unable to allow others into their lives. I believe the enemy of our souls works overtime trying to convince people to distance themselves from others in the church because Satan knows the power of becoming true members of each other.

The predominant reason people detach from the local church is that they never learn to become members of one another, as Paul said to the Romans.

For just as each of us has one body with many

members, and these members do not all have the same function, so in Christ we, though many, form one body, and each member belongs to all the others.

Romans 12:4-5

Paul makes several observations here. First, he identifies *one body in Christ.* This is the church worldwide. It is the body we all belong to as believers in Jesus Christ. Secondly, note Paul's phrase: *individually members of one of another.* Here, Paul is talking about individuals as members, and this can only happen at the level of the local church. It is the same local body referred to by the writer of Hebrews:

And let us consider how we may spur one another on toward love and good deeds, not giving up meeting together, as some are in the habit of doing, but encouraging one another—and all the more as you see the Day approaching.

Hebrews 10:24-25

People often read these verses but miss the importance of *members of one another* and *assembling of ourselves together,* thinking that as members of Christ's body, they can just follow Jesus on their own. While they can be Christians without joining with a local body of believers, in my experience, the spiritually-reclusive lifestyle doesn't work in the long run. I have seen too many people end up walking away from God, leaving Christianity, or simply stop maturing as believers. I will admit that life would be a lot easier at times if we didn't have to devote ourselves to each other in a local assembly, but for 99.99% of us, that is where the growth occurs. How many of us could claim to be good spouses if, after our wedding day, we moved to another state and never saw our wife or husband again?

Certainly would cut down on arguments, but would we really grow?

Note one of the benefits of assembling: *to provoke unto love and good works.* The author of Hebrews realized the importance of daily encouragement from each other to help combat sin in our lives. He went on to say:

> *Take care, brethren, that there not be in any one of you an evil, unbelieving heart that falls away from the living God. But encourage one another day after day, as long as it is still called "Today," so that none of you will be hardened by the deceitfulness of sin. For we have become partakers of Christ, if we hold fast the beginning of our assurance firm until the end,*

> Hebrews 3:12-14 (NASB)

Even though Jesus is our savior and His perfect word transforms us, our Christian life is not complete without other believers. Jesus designed His church to be devoted to each other's spiritual maturity. Yes, sometimes we are afraid to let others see our issues, or even to evaluate ourselves against the perfect word of God, but resisting our call to be a vital part of God's church can lead to pride and self-righteousness. It runs counter to God's requirement that we become humble and vulnerable—necessary qualities to grow into one of another.

When a jagged rock falls into a creek, years of water washing and rubbing against other rocks eventually make it round and smooth. God designed us to be members of His church where we learn to function together, gradually smoothing our rough edges.

In the same way, pulling a burning stick from a campfire extinguishers the stick's flame. It doesn't burn well apart from the other sticks. The same goes for us. Rarely can we can make it apart from a local church; we become too easily deceived and the flame of the Holy Spirit eventually goes out.

Gordon Fee, in his book *God's Empowering Presence*, says this about church and being members of one another.

> God is just not saving individuals and preparing them for heaven; rather, He is creating a people for His name, among whom God can dwell and who in their life together will reproduce God's life and character. This view of salvation is common in Paul's letters. It is evidenced nowhere more clearly than in his references to the Spirit, who plays the obvious crucial role not only in constituting the people of God, but also in their community life and worship together.
>
> The people of God as a community of believers owe their existence to their common, lavish experience of the Spirit. Thus, the question Paul answers in 1 Corinthians 12:13 is not: "How do people become believers?"—although that is being answered as well—but how do the many of them, composed of Jew and Gentile, slave and free, make up the one body of Christ. Paul's answer: all alike were immersed in the same reality, Spirit, and all alike were caused to drink to the fill of the same reality, Spirit, so as to form one body in Christ.
>
> Gordon Fee

(Fee, G. D. (1994) *God's Empowering Presence.* Peabody, Mass: Hendrickson Publishers, Inc.)

MANY PARTS

Being joined together is more than just an act of our wills, however. As followers of Christ, we supernaturally become members of Jesus' church through the Holy Spirit, being called as members of one another. Membership into His body is foundational to everything we will do in Christianity. It is essential for understanding the heart of God and His intentions for His people.

> *Just as one body, though one, has many parts, but all its many parts form one body, so it is with Christ. For we were all baptized by one Spirit so as to form one body—whether Jews or Gentiles, slave or free—and we were all given the one Spirit to drink. Even so the body is not made up of one part but of many.*
>
> 1 Corinthians 12:12-14

> *For as in one body we have many members, and the members do not all have the same function, so we, though many, are one body in Christ, and individually members one of another.*
>
> Romans 12:4-5 (NASB)

The biblical definition of *member* is derived from the differing members of the physical body. Each member has a God-ordained function that supports the functioning of the entire body. Yet, we can only function as a spiritual body if we submit to God and His design for the church, being joined to each other in the spirit of unity.

If, as a member of Christ's body, I purposely neglect my connection with others, I am telling God and my fellow Christians:

- I don't need them.
- I don't want to be what God designed.

23

- I'm fine on my own.

There are many reasons Christians hold these attitudes and stay disconnected from a local body of believers.

- Fear of vulnerability.

- Guilt and shame.

- Past hurts and fear of trusting people.

- Thinking they don't need help.

- Want to be left alone.

- Rebellion to the call of God.

As Americans, we feel we have the right to choose everything in our lives. While this can be beneficial in some areas, it also leads to church-hopping and refusing to devote ourselves to a local church. Yet God's plan is that each member submit to local authority and be joined one to another under leadership.

At the same time, the leadership of any given church must be led by the Holy Spirit. Leadership cannot use its position in a local body to abuse, control, or dominate God's precious people. Accountability goes both ways.

Let's face it: Being joined one to another is not easy. Fortunately, Jesus has an answer to help us function as vital members of God's church. In fact, He *is* the answer. He is our model for leading people with authority and loving them while staying aligned with the Father's will. It all comes down to living love. If we are empowered by the Holy Spirit, we will seek to do His will, which is to glorify Jesus and build His church.

We are more than saved beings walking alone with God. We are truly our brothers' and sisters' keepers. We are to look out for each other, help each other, pray for each other, speak the truth to each other, and build each other up. There is never a time in our Christian life where we graduate *out* of God's body. If you are saved, you are part of Christ's body. And just as human body parts don't disconnect and run around on their own, believers are to remain connected for a purpose—to help the body of Christ function as God intended.

While every believer is a part of Christ's body, the local church is a microcosm of that body. The body of Christ is comprised of local churches, which are comprised of you...and others like you. The local church is our model for how the body of Christ should operate. Jesus is the head of His body and the head of local bodies. When we neglect the local church, we are actually neglecting the headship of Jesus. Salvation is the beginning of our relationship with Christ; growth in a local body is the continuation of our maturity in Christ.

God designed His church for fellowship both among believers and with Him. He seeks to dwell among His people, causing them to encourage each other and hold each other accountable—members loving fellow members so we can all grow into the likeness of Jesus. When sinners see Christians loving each other as Jesus did, they will be drawn to us.

> *By this everyone will know that you are my disciples,*
> *if you love one another.*

> John 13:35 (NASB)

In the early church, people were saved daily because God dwelled with His people and the people were devoted to God's purpose and each other. It should be so even now.

> *They devoted themselves to the apostles' teaching*
> *and to fellowship, to the breaking of bread and to*
> *prayer. Everyone was filled with awe at the many*

wonders and signs performed by the apostles. All the believers were together and had everything in common. They sold property and possessions to give to anyone who had need. Every day they continued to meet together in the temple courts. They broke bread in their homes and ate together with glad and sincere hearts, praising God and enjoying the favor of all the people. And the Lord added to their number daily those who were being saved.

Acts 2:42-47

MY STORY

God designed His kingdom to be a community of people connected through the Holy Spirit—loving, encouraging, and building each other up. Lori and I went to a great church pastored by Dick Iversen from 1991 through 1994, called Bible Temple, in Portland, Oregon. This is where we began to learn what it meant to be members in a great church

In 1997, Lori and I met with Bob and Sue MacGregor at City Harvest Church. Our experience at City Harvest Church with Pastor Bob was an even greater experience because we were on the ground floor of the church plant in 1998. City Harvest Church was where we saw God work through others to help us fulfill our destiny. It was also where we learned to help others fulfill their destiny in Christ.

Lori and I will never forget what Pastor Bob said to us on that first visit over lunch. He said, "I am not looking for you to come here so I can build a church with your gifts. I am looking for you to come here so I can watch God develop your gifts which will help you find your destiny in Christ." Pastor Bob was more concerned about people growing in their gifts and talents than he was about building an empire for himself. Pastor Bob helped us learn ministry, helped us in our marriage, helped us parent our kids, and helped us have faith for our future.

During our 12+ years at City Harvest Church, we saw the good, the bad, and the ugly when it comes to ministry and the local church. What keeps us going in ministry today is seeing Jesus take undeserving people like us and give them beauty for ashes. When people get the true revelation of God's church, they begin to help others follow Jesus. When church leadership loves and serves people, it encourages them to do the same.

In 1987, Jesus entered my dorm room and showed me what it means to love others. But it was the 12 years at City Harvest Church that taught me what love looked like. True church community happens when we never forget how God healed our brokenness through the love of others. This is how we become members of one another.

APPLICATION

Let's ask Jesus to transform our hearts and minds to His word. As we look into God's perfect word, let's honestly evaluate if we are committed and submitted to it. As we ask God to fill us with more of His Spirit, we must crucify the things that rise up in our flesh that are contrary to His word.

> *Therefore, having put away falsehood, let each one of you speak the truth with his neighbor, for we are members one of another.*
>
> Ephesians 4:25 (ESV)
>
> *And he is before all things, and in him all things hold together. And he is the head of the body, the church.*

he is the beginning, the firstborn from the dead, that in everything he might be preeminent.

Colossians 1:17-18 (ESV)

For it stands in scripture: "Behold, I am laying in Zion a stone, a cornerstone chosen and precious, and whoever believes in him will not be put to shame." So the honor is for you who believe, but for those who do not believe, "The stone that the builders rejected has become the cornerstone," and "A stone of stumbling, and a rock of offense." They stumble because they disobey the word, as they were destined to do. But you are a chosen race, a royal priesthood, a holy nation, a people for his own possession, that you may proclaim the excellences' of him who called you out of darkness into his marvelous light. Once you were not a people, but now you are God's people; once you had not received mercy, but now you have received mercy.

1 Peter 2:6-10 (ESV)

Consequently, you are no longer foreigners and strangers, but fellow citizens with God's people and also members of his household, built on the foundation of the apostles and prophets, with Christ Jesus himself as the chief cornerstone. In him the whole building is joined together and rises to become a holy temple in the Lord. And in him you too are being built together to become a dwelling in which God lives by his Spirit.

Ephesians 2:19-22

Members of One Another

Let's be honest.

If you are afraid to function as a member of a local church, Jesus can help you. If you don't trust people, ask Jesus to uncover the roots of that mistrust. He can heal you and fill you with His love. He removes all fear. It might take forgiving those in your past who hurt you. You might be afraid to become devoted to a local church because of a past church leadership that was abusive. Perhaps you swore to never connect deeply to a church again. Well, Jesus can heal you of that condition as well. Church leaders are not perfect. They can be insecure and make mistakes; they are no different than you on the inside. They need healing and forgiveness as well. Jesus said there would be many false teachers and leaders that are only after their own good and not the good of the sheep. If you are a part of a church where you feel spiritually abused or controlled, or if you feel the leadership is not as loving as Jesus, then ask God to give you wisdom and direction.

On the other hand, maybe you are rebellious and want to call the shots in your life. In that case, ask Jesus to search your heart for the source of your rebellion. If you are honest with Jesus, He will be faithful and just to forgive and heal you. Jesus understands that you have sin in your life; He came to take away your sin, deliver you from all your fears, and give you freedom. In return, He asks for honesty.

I encourage you to take the necessary time to seek God with all your heart, being filled with the Holy Spirit and walking in the power of God's grace. The importance of being continually filled with the Holy Spirit cannot be over-emphasized.

Here is a quote from John G. Lake on the importance of the baptism in the Holy Spirit and what happens when Jesus Himself enters your body.

> The Baptism of the Holy Ghost is not an influence, nor yet a good feeling, nor sweet sensations, though it may include all of these. The Baptism of the Holy Ghost is the incoming into the personality of Him, the Holy Ghost, which is in direct conflict with your (mind and animal life), yea, of your flesh. He possesses the being. The flesh is caused to quake sometimes because of the presence of the Spirit of God in the flesh. Daniel quaked with great quaking when the Spirit of the Lord came upon him (Daniel 10:1-13).

> Beloved reader, do you realize that it is the Spirit of Jesus who is seeking admittance into your heart and life? Do you realize that it is the Spirit of Jesus within the spirit, soul, and body of the baptized believer Who moves him in ways sometimes strange, but Who accomplishes the wondrous work of God within the life. That is why every baptized believer praises God for what has taken place in him.

> John G Lake

As we examine ourselves against the scriptures and ask Jesus to search our hearts, He takes all our hurts, mistrust, anxiety, depression, shame, guilt, and fear upon His shoulders. He gives us more of the Holy Spirit's peace and joy so we can function as precious members of His church. Jesus is passionate about connecting us as a church because there are many more people that Jesus wants to bring into His church. We are the key to getting others saved and connected.

When it comes to walking in the Spirit and crucifying the flesh, Jesus gave His followers the power to pray and resist the devil. Satan tells us we don't deserve to be free in Christ; he deceives us into hiding in our hurts, shame, guilt, and fear. He tempts us with inferiority or superiority by comparing ourselves to others. But the truth is, he is a liar and the father of lies.

> *You belong to your father, the devil, and you want to carry out your father's desires. He was a murderer from the beginning, not holding to the truth, for there is no truth in him. When he lies, he speaks his native language, for he is a liar and the father of lies.*
>
> John 8:44

As you pray and study the scriptures in this chapter, consider starting with this prayer:

"Father, in Jesus' name, I submit to You. I resist the enemy and he has to flee from me and leave me alone."

Satan will respond because he must answer to the name of Jesus.

SELF-EVALUATION OR GROUP DISCUSSION

- How does the building described in Ephesians 2 compare to a physical structure built by people?

- Considering the supernatural act of God in placing us into His church. What does that say about the importance of being committed to a community of believers? Explain

- The Bible compares the body of Christ to our physical body, so imagine you are the eyes and you decide to quit working—you just decide to quit and leave. How would that affect the body?

Live Love

- How does the church show the world that it is the dwelling place of the Spirit of God?

  o Hint: read Acts 2:42-47 again before you answer.

  o Do you see these characteristics displayed in your church? Explain.

- When you see new people at church, how do you respond?

- How do you think Jesus would greet you on a Sunday morning if you were new in His church?

- What are the ramifications of acknowledging that the church is a dwelling in which God lives by His Spirit?

- What are some personal obstacles that keep you from being devoted to others in your local church?

- Are there past hurts, pains, and offenses that keep you from being devoted to God and His church? Ask the Holy Spirit to show you anything that keeps you from being vulnerable and accountable to others. List them out as the Lord shows you.

- Since becoming members of one another is a supernatural act of God similar to marriage, where He makes two people one, how do you treat your spouse, kids, and extended family, knowing that God united all of you in the Spirit?

- Based on God's word in this chapter and His love for His church, how would you rate yourself on a scale of 1-5 (1=bad 5=very good) when it comes to you obeying God's word about being members of one another? Explain.

- What are you doing to change so you align with God's word?

JOURNAL

I encourage you to journal everything the Lord speaks to you concerning His will of being members of one another. Remember that the Holy Spirit is gracious and loving and will guide you into all truth. Repentance is not a punishment; it is releasing you to live love.

Write down your fears and ask God why you have these fears. As you begin to face your fears and give them to God, He will replace them with love and a sound mind of Christ. There are reasons we have fears and insecurities. Jesus can heal them all.

PRAYER

Father, in Jesus Name, I repent of any heart attitudes that would keep me from obeying Your word. I confess that God's word is perfect and He has designed me to function as a member of His church body. I submit to God's will in Jesus name. Lord Jesus, if there is anything in my heart that is keeping me from living out Acts 2:24-47 as You prescribed, then I ask the Holy Spirit and Your word to show me what it is. I submit to Your word and will work on being a true member of God's holy church. Jesus, I really need Your help right now to get over the pain of past offenses. Please help me.

Father, I also ask to be baptized afresh in the Holy Spirit so I can be empowered to be members of one another the way You have called us to be. Holy Spirit, flood my being right now with Your Holy Presence. Amen.

Live Love

<u>NOTES</u>

3

Building Up One Another

Therefore encourage one another and build each other up, just as in fact you are doing.

1 Thessalonians 5:11

To *build up* means to increase the potential of someone. Maybe they're broken, depressed, or confused. Maybe their self-esteem is crushed. Whatever their condition, they can't see themselves as God sees them. And that's where the church comes in.

Do not let any unwholesome talk come out of your mouths, but only what is helpful for building others up according to their needs, that it may benefit those who listen.

Ephesians 4:29

God calls each member of His church to commit to *building others up.* Fortunately for us, Jesus provided a map for what He wants His Church to look like, detailing how we are to act.

So Christ himself gave the apostles, the prophets, the evangelists, the pastors and teachers, to equip his people for works of service, so that the body of Christ

*may be built up until we all reach unity in the faith
and in the knowledge of the Son of God and become
mature, attaining to the whole measure of the fullness
of Christ. Then we will no longer be infants, tossed
back and forth by the waves, and blown here and
there by every wind of teaching and by the cunning
and craftiness of people in their deceitful scheming.
Instead, speaking the truth in love, we will grow
to become in every respect the mature body of him
who is the head, that is, Christ. From him the whole
body, joined and held together by every supporting
ligament, grows and builds itself up in love, as each
part does its work.*

Ephesians 4:11-16

Imagine a church that was consistently building each other up and providing for each other's needs. Who or what could successfully come against it? It could withstand anything. We the church encounter people from all walks of life, backgrounds, world views, and conditions. How we minister to them determines our effectiveness to live love.

Here is a testimony on the subject by Amy Wonch, a single mom in our church, who has recently come to Christ:

What does *live love* mean to me?

To drop it all, all the anger, all the hurt and sadness and know that in the very midst of all the brokenness seeing that it's His love that draws us closer to Him and one another, in such a way that we breathe as one and serve and worship as one true glorious body bringing His name the highest of praise.

The last few months have been very challenging and earth-shaking for me, but at the moment of my deepest pain, Jesus picked my dirty torn heart up off the floor and came closer to me and with overwhelming grace in His eyes, He placed a new heart safely into my chest and I feel it is a beautiful and holy part of Him that now beats inside of me. His challenge was to strengthen and test my faith, and with time, He continues to give me more courage to love and encourage others as they take the steps of their faith. He is showing me where my heart is truly examined and where we find our true love and fellowship for Him.

Amy Wonch

BUILD YOU UP

Now I commit you to God and to the word of his grace, which can build you up and give you an inheritance among all those who are sanctified.

Acts 20:32

Jesus knew exactly what He was doing by building His Church. He knew that broken people would need restoration by the power of the Holy Spirit. So, in one of the great mysteries of the church, Jesus determined to use broken people to restore other broken people. We are called to build each other up—to mature and grow together in love—despite our own conditions.

In the Old Testament, God called Israel—the smallest of nations—to make disciples of all other nations. Israel was God's chosen and broken people sent to influence the world. God is still calling His broken people today to build and encourage others so we can grow together in His love. The more we grow as members of one another, building each other up, the more outsiders will come to be with us—a community of believers that live love.

> *We who are strong ought to bear with the failings of the weak and not to please ourselves. ² Each of us should please our neighbors for their good, to build them up. ³ For even Christ did not please himself but, as it is written: "The insults of those who insult you have fallen on me." ⁴ For everything that was written in the past was written to teach us, so that through the endurance taught in the scriptures and the encouragement they provide we might have hope.*

> Romans 15:1-4

KEY PEOPLE

I have known great mentors who invested their lives in me. Pastor Bob McGregor and Pastor Dave Minor were two people that I could go to and ask anything I wanted, knowing I would get their love and respect in return. They taught me about ministry, marriage, how to pastor people, and how to love. As my pastors and friends, they also had permission to ask me tough questions about how I was doing in life. When they did, I knew it was for my benefit. They wanted to see me grow in Christ and increase my potential as a future lead pastor.

Nate and Monique McGoldrick helped us start City Life Church (now Living Stone Church) in 2010 when they were a young family. They followed us over to Spokane, WA from City Harvest Church in Vancouver, WA, which is our sending church. Nate and Monique have four young children and have learned to live love. Here is a testimonial from them.

Living Love is such a wonderful thing to say. The sweet taste of the phrase is almost palpable as it rolls off the tongue. Yes, let us live out love, as long as everyone else is doing it and I get to keep acting in my own best interests! One of the very tangible ways that we can learn to truly live out love is in the context of the family. It is here that all facades tend to melt away and we know the true character of our spouses and our sons and daughters. A few years back we came to the realization that we weren't building each other up in our family. We were nit-picky and constantly criticizing each other for failures to perform. We noticed a real hesitance in our children and ourselves to take risks in relationships because we hadn't spent time nurturing confidence. It was through the continual prompting of the Holy Spirit and our pastor's presentation of the word of God that we finally turned the corner and began to encourage each other. Our home now is a peaceful place, where love is flourishing and fear of failure is subsiding. We have grown leaps and bounds in our ability to live out love all because we decided to build each other up instead of tear each other down. This atmosphere has also begun to flow out of our home into our workplace, our community, and our local church. Even more confirmation of the power of this change is seeing this outlook replicated in our children. Just recently one of our children was prophesied over that they would be an encouraging voice to all their friends. Let the words of this chapter sink deeply in and join our family in living out love by building up one another!

MY STORY

A key to living love is to be honest with God about the parts of our flesh that need to be dealt with.

One of the biggest obstacles in my life, before and after I met Christ, was that my dad never taught me how to love. In truth, he didn't know how to love. He was a good man overall, and I certainly don't have major complaints about my upbringing, but Dad didn't know how to love. He especially did not know how to love my mom. He wasn't abusive; he was just a reclusive man who internalized his pain and couldn't give what he didn't have. During my 18 years of childhood, I cannot recall one time that he encouraged or built up Mom. I saw its effect on her and knew I couldn't be like that. I needed a lot of help in this area.

When I was saved in 1987, God led me to confront my lack of godly love for others, especially women. It didn't help that I was a college football star in the eyes of the non-players. In truth, I was only average, but still, everyone looked up to me. I didn't have to work hard for their admiration because they didn't know the real me. When Lori and I started dating, however, I was terrified. What did it mean to be a boyfriend or even a husband? I spent a lot of time on my knees asking God to fill me with His Spirit. I searched His word to change my heart. I lived (and still live) Hebrews 4:12-13, allowing God's word to penetrate every aspect of my being. During that time, I learned that my greatest strength was my weakness; I was honest with God about my lack in this area. I had to be. I knew if I didn't allow His word to penetrate my heart, my future marriage would fail. And God worked in my life.

Today we live in blissful marital harmony. Well...almost. We are real people with real faults and strengths. But best of all, we are real with ourselves, each other, and God. I've learned to love, understanding first and foremost that love does not require perfection to lead us to perfection; that warts and blemishes are part of God's plan; that the love that tolerates mistakes and shortcomings is greater than the love that permits none of these. We have learned to accept each other in Christ for who we are, always striving to bring out the best in each other.

Sometimes, people think it's OK to harbor bad attitudes, hatred, bitterness or unforgiveness. Unfortunately, these hidden sins often become the excuse for not building up others. I call this "stinking thinking." As a Christian man, I am called to love my wife and build her up. According to God's word, I don't have a choice. I am commanded to love her. This drove me to God, seeking healing for the way Dad raised me. In the process, I also forgave him for his example as a husband. In fact, there was such a deep disconnect in my life regarding loving others that I still work on it today, 30 years after Jesus walked into my life and changed me forever. At the time, He said He'd show me what it means to love people the way He loves them. And today, the lesson continues, to the glory of God.

RESTORED

Neil Anderson, in his book titled *Restored*, shares an important key in helping us live love.

> Building one another up requires freedom in Christ;
> there can be no offense, bitterness or unforgiveness
> toward each other. As we allow God to cleanse us,
> we are free to restore one another.

Those who have truly helped others experience their freedom in Christ will testify that forgiveness of others is the primary issue that needs to be resolved. Unforgiveness by Christians afford Satan his greatest access to the church, and many believers are bound to the past because they have failed to forgive others as Christ has forgiven them.

Some people react negatively to the idea of forgiving others because they see it as another form of victimization. It goes against their sense of justice. "Oh, sure, just forgive and keep getting slapped around!" They believe it is a sign of weakness, the continuation of the sickening saga of co-dependency.

On the contrary, forgiveness is a courageous act that reflects the grace of God. Forgiveness is not tolerating sin. God forgives, but he doesn't tolerate sin. Therefore, scriptural boundaries must be set up to stop further abuse. Forgiving others is something you do for your sake, and resistance breaks down when you understand what it is and how to do it.

Neil Anderson

(Anderson, N. T. *Restored: Experience Life With Jesus*. Franklin, TN. e3 Resource, 2007)

APPLICATIONS

If you find it hard to connect to others in church, it will be impossible to build others up. Now is the time to be honest with God and admit Him into the areas of your life that prevent you from being a builder and encourager of others. Jesus knows every detail of your life. He knows your negative thoughts, pain, and offenses—everything you think is hidden. His answer to you is that He offers you living water to cleanse every negative thing in your life. But here's the catch. He can't *take* the bad things from you. Instead, you must *give* them to Him. Then He can give you forgiveness, love, gentleness, peace, and joy in the power of the Holy Spirit. Yes, He forgives your sin at salvation, but there are some things we must purposely cut off in our lives. We are not working to earn God's love; we are working *in* His love, yearning to remove all that would stand between our lives and His abundant life.

The good news is that when Jesus calls us to live love and build others up, He also provides the power to do so. The enemy tries to build divisions among us: jealousy, envy, fear, and suspicion, making it difficult to encourage each other. If you find obstacles in your life as I did in mine when I tried to love Lori, consider the prayer at the end of this chapter. Of course, praying a single prayer isn't going to fix all your problems, but it will get you started on the road of healing if you are honest before God. It worked for me; it can work for all of us.

Our goal as members of Christ's body is to learn to speak life and encouragement into people, increasing their potential as followers of Christ and ultimately catapulting them to do the same to others. As Christians belonging to a local church, connected to the body of Christ, ushering in the Kingdom of God throughout the world, our vision must extend beyond ourselves. He saved us to help save others.

Therefore encourage one another and build each other up, just as in fact you are doing.

1 Thessalonians 5:11

Live Love

Because anyone who serves Christ in this way is pleasing to God and receives human approval. Let us therefore make every effort to do what leads to peace and to mutual edification.

Romans 14:18-19

- Think about a time when someone recognized your potential and invested in you.

  o How did this make you feel?

  o How are you different today because of this person's investment and encouragement in your life?

- What are some areas at your church where people are successfully building each other up?

- How does encouragement help build others? What are some ways you can encourage in word, attitude, and action?

- When new people come to your church and see people being built up and encouraged by each other, what do you think they will tell their friends?

- How can this biblical principle of building each other up be used in helping people come to Christ? Explain.

- As a member of your local church, how can you help make it a place that builds others up instead of causing others to stumble?

- Do you know a fellow student or co-worker who could benefit from someone building them up? Write down the name and make a plan to encourage and build them up.

- As a husband or wife, what are you doing to build up your spouse daily? Explain.

- As a parent, how are you increasing the potential of your kids so they can be more like Christ? Give examples.

- Many people grew up in homes filled with strife and negativity. We naturally tend to do what our parent(s) or guardians did to us. Since God's word commands us to build up and encourage each other, how do we deal with our negative past?

- On a scale of 1-5, how would rate yourself on building up your family, friends, coworkers, church family, and others that are in weekly contact with you?

- Do you speak life or death to your siblings, parents, kids, and friends?

- What steps are you taking to change based on the scriptures in this chapter?

- As a pastor, elder, staff pastor, worship leader, small group leader, or office staff in a church, are you building your team up and increasing the potential of each person?

- As a leader in the church, do you find yourself focusing more on building your area of ministry or building others?

- As a Christian leader in the workplace, are you building up and increasing the potential of all, including the non-Christians?

JOURNAL

I encourage you to write everything of which the scriptures in this chapter have convicted you or encouraged you. Continue to write your fears and how God is replacing them with His love. Never forget the things that can supernaturally transform your life: God's Spirit mixed with His perfect word, and being members of each other. I also encourage you to share with a friend what God did in your life through this chapter. Remember, you have friends, family, coworkers, and associates who need to be built up and encouraged to serve Jesus. The greatest way to bring others to Jesus is to let them see how Jesus changed your life.

PRAYER

Father, I come to You in Jesus name. I know Your word says that I am supposed to build others up and encourage them, but I have such a hard time doing that. I am asking that You come and fill me with Your love and mercy so I can reach out and encourage. I repent of any bitterness, hatred, envy, strife, jealousy, and unforgiveness that would hinder me from being used by You to build and encourage Your church. If there is a situation in my life where I was offended, hurt, or abused in some way that I don't remember, I ask You, Father, to remind me so I can forgive and move on. I submit my life to Your words that I have read in this chapter and ask that the Holy Spirit penetrates every area in my life. Father, I also ask for a fresh baptism in the Holy Spirit. Flood my life with Your power and love. I need You, Jesus, to come in and cleanse me from all of my past. Amen.

NOTES

Live Love

4

Love One Another

The end of all things is near. Therefore be alert and of sober mind so that you may pray. Above all, love each other deeply, because love covers over a multitude of sins. Offer hospitality to one another without grumbling.

1 Peter 4:7-9

Peter was one of Jesus' closest disciples. He was the first to identify Jesus as the Christ. And when God poured out His Spirit on Pentecost, Peter was the first to speak up, preaching a message that brought 3000 people to salvation through Jesus Christ. Later, while walking with John, Peter brought healing to a lame man, famously declaring: *"Silver or gold I do not have, but what I do have I give you. In the name of Jesus Christ of Nazareth, walk"* (Acts 3).

Yes, Peter was doing great things in God. However, God was about to do great things in Peter.

The first clue of God's intention for Peter's life came in Acts 8. The Holy Spirit was working in Samaria through Phillip the Evangelist, and Peter and John were sent to be witnesses. This was remarkable because the Jews and Samaritans were bitter enemies at the time. Even more remarkable is that Peter and John laid hands on the Samaritans in prayer and they received the Holy Spirit.

This encounter could not have been easy for Peter—a staunch Jew before meeting Jesus, and now an apostle still clinging to his Jewish roots. Of course, that was before God gave him a vision and sent him to the house of Cornelius to minister to the Gentiles gathered there. This was initially repugnant to Peter, as the Gentiles were considered pagans and unclean by the Jews. Yet God had a plan and the Holy Spirit was given to these Gentile believers through Peter's ministry.

Upon returning to Jerusalem, Peter faced a backlash from the other Jewish-based believers for his association with Gentiles. His explanation to his accusers, as given in Acts 11, says it all.

> The apostles and the believers throughout Judea heard that the Gentiles also had received the word of God. ² So when Peter went up to Jerusalem, the circumcised believers criticized him ³ and said, "You went into the house of uncircumcised men and ate with them." ⁴ Starting from the beginning, Peter told them the whole story: ⁵ "I was in the city of Joppa praying, and in a trance I saw a vision. I saw something like a large sheet being let down from heaven by its four corners, and it came down to where I was. ⁶ I looked into it and saw four-footed animals of the earth, wild beasts, reptiles and birds. ⁷ Then I heard a voice telling me, 'Get up, Peter. Kill and eat.'
>
> ⁸ "I replied, 'Surely not, Lord! Nothing impure or unclean has ever entered my mouth.'
>
> ⁹ "The voice spoke from heaven a second time, 'Do

not call anything impure that God has made clean.'[10]
This happened three times, and then it was all pulled
up to heaven again.

Acts 11:1-10

Such an impactful demonstration of God's perspective regarding clean and unclean was necessary for Peter because of the deep-seated dislike and national Jewish pride the Jewish believers had against the Gentiles.

Although he was with Jesus from the beginning and witnessed firsthand God's love for Jews, Samaritans, Gentiles, rich, poor, sick, broken, and demon possessed, Peter never fully accepted the deep love that he describes in his letter (1 Peter 4) until years after his conversion. Even hearing Jesus cry out from the cross, *"Father, forgive them for they do not know what they are doing,"* (Luke 23:34), was not enough to fully change Peter's heart. Yes, he had a new love in his heart when he preached boldly at Pentecost. But through this vision of the clean and unclean, Jesus was showing Peter that he still did not love deeply enough to win over his enemies. Peter was fine pastoring his fellow Jewish converts, but he didn't love the Samaritans and Gentiles as Jesus did. The "deep love" didn't fully come to fruition until a few years after his baptism in the Spirit at Pentecost.

If there is one message that God wants for us above all else, it is to *love more deeply.*

> *"By this everyone will know that you are my disciples,*
> *if you love one another."*

John 13:35

MY STORY

I had a similar experience to Peter's. I grew up on the Colville Indian Reservation as a white person—my parents were both white. Being in an area of 90% Native Americans, I was called "Honky" a lot. I was even roughed up a few times—kicked, punched, and slammed to the ground. This started in grade school and built up over the years. Now I have to admit, this was only by a few of my schoolmates. And I wasn't assaulted *every* day with name calling and beatings, but it did build a hatred in my heart towards a few Native Americans. Still, most were very good friends and we had no issues between us.

As we grew into high school, there were still that handful of Natives that called me "Honky" and continued to make me feel an outcast. Consequently, when I left the Reservation for college, I had a deep-rooted hatred for a few people on the Reservation. Again, I had many friends who were Native, so I didn't have a blanket hatred for all Natives, but my heart wasn't right and I felt I had good reason to hate a few of them back.

Two years later when I got saved and filled with the Spirit of God, Jesus did a complete surgery on my heart for the people for whom I had hatred. It was as if God showed me the same thing He showed Peter—that He doesn't create junk. Sometimes in our lives, we feel we have an excuse to hate because we were hurt, but God put a love in me that was supernatural, just as He did with Peter for the Samaritans and the Gentiles. Since 1987, when I look at any people group, my heart cries out for their salvation. I know now that the people calling me "Honky" and saying I was unwelcome on their land were acting out of ignorance. Jesus taught us what to do when He prayed: *"Father, forgive them, for they do not know what they are doing"* (Luke 23:34).

Jesus healed the hurt, anger, and hatred I had for my fellow man because He loves all people. He doesn't make junk. All people are created in the image of God and need to know Him.

BY YOUR LOVE

The defining mark of Jesus' disciples is their love for one another. When the church succeeds in showing Christ-like love, our neighborhoods, cities, and nations will know we belong to Jesus. Stephen demonstrated that love as he was being stoned to death by the Jews, praying as Jesus did: *"Lord Jesus, receive my spirit." Then he fell on his knees and cried out, "Lord, do not hold this sin against them"* (Acts 7:59-60).

The ultimate form of love is realizing that God's will and salvation are more important than our lives. Peter realized this when he finally understood that Jesus loved the Samaritans and Gentiles as much as He loved the Jews. Stephen, while dying an agonizing death, realized that the salvation of his fellow Jews was more important than saving his own life.

When we receive Christ and are filled with the Holy Spirit, we no longer own our lives. 1 Corinthians 6:19-20 says: *Do you not know that your bodies are temples of the Holy Spirit, who is in you, whom you have received from God? You are not your own; you were bought at a price. Therefore honor God with your bodies.* God's desire is that we see people as He sees them, with our hearts filled with the same compassion as His—the same deep love.

Here is a powerful excerpt from a sermon that John G Lake

preached in the early 1900s. He speaks of the true baptism in the spirit and how it should produce the love of Jesus in us over any signs or manifestations:

> The baptism in the Spirit produced in me a love for mankind such as I had never comprehended in my life. Yea, a soul yearning to see men saved, so deep, at times heart-rending, until in anguish of soul I was compelled to abandon my business and turn all my attention to bringing men to the feet of Jesus. While this process was going on in my heart, during a period of months, sometimes persons would come into my office to transact business and even instances where there were great profits to be had for a few minutes of persistent application to business, the Spirit of Love in me so yearned over souls that I could not even see the profits to be had. Under its sway money lost its value to me, and in many instances, I found myself utterly unable to talk business to the individual until first I had poured out the love passion of my soul and endeavored to show him Jesus as his then present Savior. In not just a few instances these business engagements ended in the individual yielding himself to God.

> That love passion for men's souls has sometimes been overshadowed by the weight of care since then, but only for a moment. Again, when occasion demanded it, that mighty love flame absorbing one's whole being and life would flame forth until, under the anointing of the Holy Ghost on many occasions,

sinners would fall in my arms and yield their hearts to God.

Others have sought for evidences of the Pentecostal experience being the real Baptism of the Holy Ghost. Some have criticized and said, "It is not a delusion?" In all the scale of evidences presented to my soul and taken from my experience, this experience of the divine love, the burning love and holy compassion of Jesus Christ filling one's bosom until no sacrifice is too great to win a soul for Christ, demonstrates to me more than any other one thing that this is indeed none other than the Spirit of Jesus.

Such love is not human! Such love is only divine! Such love is only Jesus Himself, who gave His life for others.

John G Lake

APPLICATION

- Is there a difference between the biblical understanding of love and the worldly understanding of love?
- What do you see as being the major differences between the two viewpoints?
- Why is the world in love with worldly love?
- How would you describe Christ-like love?
- Do most people think of Christians as being loving people?

Now may our God and Father himself and our Lord Jesus clear the way for us to come to you. May the

Live Love

Lord make your love increase and overflow for each other and for everyone else, just as ours does for you.

1 Thessalonians 3:11-12

Now about your love for one another we do not need to write to you, for you yourselves have been taught by God to love each other. And in fact, you do love all of God's family throughout Macedonia. Yet we urge you, brothers and sisters, to do so more and more

1 Thessalonians 4:9-10

We ought always to thank God for you, brothers and sisters, and rightly so, because your faith is growing more and more, and the love all of you have for one another is increasing.

2 Thessalonians 1:3

- What is the source of all love?

  o What does that mean for us as Christians?

- Paul wrote that the Thessalonians were taught by God to love one another. Why is the truth of scripture the foundation for understanding how to love?

  o What it means to be loved?

- The Thessalonian's love extended beyond Thessalonica to the churches in Macedonia.

  o How does the love of your local church shine in your city and beyond?

  o Why should Christian love always radiate outward into the world?

- What unique opportunities has God set before you to show

His love to the people around you? Take time and ask God to show you and then write them down.

- Jesus has given us the cure for our separation from God and the sickness called sin—His name is Jesus. Is it loving for you and me to have the cure of salvation and not give it to people around us?

For this very reason, make every effort to add to your faith goodness; and to goodness, knowledge; and to knowledge, self-control; and to self-control, perseverance; and to perseverance, godliness; and to godliness, mutual affection; and to mutual affection, love. For if you possess these qualities in increasing measure, they will keep you from being ineffective and unproductive in your knowledge of our Lord Jesus Christ.

2 Peter 1:5-8

Let no debt remain outstanding, except the continuing debt to love one another, for whoever loves others has fulfilled the law. The commandments, "You shall not commit adultery," "You shall not murder," "You shall not steal," "You shall not covet," and whatever other command there may be, are summed up in this one command: "Love your neighbor as yourself." Love does no harm to a neighbor. Therefore love is the fulfillment of the law.

Romans 13:8-10

- How does my life reflect these scriptures?
- Think of someone or maybe a group of people that you

normally would ignore. What simple steps could you take to show them an act of love this week?

- When you evaluate your life against the scriptures above, what are some reasons it might be hard for you to love others deeply?

- How would you rate yourself in loving your family, friends, coworkers, and church family more than yourself?

- Write down areas that you need the Holy Spirit to help you when it comes to loving people more deeply.

- Are you shedding your fears and replacing them with God's love?

- Love begins at home. What are you doing to love your spouse more deeply? Explain in detail (but keep it PG).

One of the reasons Jesus was and is the most loving person to ever live is because He knows the difference between heaven and hell. He has witnessed countless people who choose to reject His salvation and He sees them suffering in hell. He loves so deeply that He hung on a cross and received the full wrath of God for you and me. Because of our sin and rebellion, we deserve an eternity in hell; but Jesus loved so deeply that He took our punishment from God and gave us abundant life.

JOURNAL

Journal, journal, journal! Write down everything Jesus is speaking to you about loving deeply and forgiving others. If you allow it, Jesus will flood your heart and mind with things to write down that pertain to the scriptures in this chapter. Also, keep coming back to the scriptures and allow God's perfect word to transform your heart and mind to look more and more like Jesus' heart and mind. Remember that Jesus loves us so deeply that He paid for all of our sin and rebellion on the cross.

PRAYER

Father, infuse me with the same love that You love with. I ask, by the power of the Holy Spirit, that You give me a new level of love for others that is impossible for me to do on my own. I also ask, Lord, that I learn to hate the world system of control and power, instead loving only You and Your kingdom. Father, I look at these scriptures and I ask that You help me apply them to every area of my life: my family, friends, and every stranger I meet. Help me to love people that don't love me. Amen.

Jesus, I also ask You to help me forgive the people in my life who have hurt me, wounded me, and abused me. I ask You to take the hate that is in my heart towards them and turn it into love. It is impossible for me to think that I could love the people that have hurt me, but Your word says nothing is impossible with You. Please flood me with Your love. Please turn my bitterness and hate into unconditional love toward my enemies.

Pray this if it applies to you.

Father, I feel abandoned, betrayed and neglected by others. I tell myself that I am going to reach out to others but all I feel is pain. I end up hiding and masking who I am. I need healing in this area, Lord. I want to forgive my parents and anyone in authority who may have influenced these feelings. I need Your help. Please heal my broken and abandoned heart. Amen.

Live Love

NOTES

5

Pursue Good and Not Evil

<And> I have the same hope in God as these men themselves have, that there will be a resurrection of both the righteous and the wicked. So I strive always to keep my conscience clear before God and man.

Acts 24:15-16

The Apostle Paul suffered as much or more than any human has ever suffered. If ever a person had excuses to repay evil for evil, it was Paul. Check out his life of dire circumstances endured as he proclaimed the gospel of Jesus Christ to an unbelieving world.

We give no offense in anything, that our ministry may not be blamed. ⁴ But in all things we commend ourselves as ministers of God: in much <u>patience,</u> in <u>tribulations,</u> in <u>needs,</u> in <u>distresses,</u> ⁵ in <u>stripes,</u> in <u>imprisonments,</u> in <u>tumults,</u> in <u>labors,</u> in <u>sleeplessness,</u> in <u>fasting's;</u> ⁶ by purity, by knowledge, by <u>long suffering,</u> by kindness, by the Holy Spirit, by sincere love, ⁷ by the word of truth, by the power of God, by the armor of righteousness on the right hand and on the left, ⁸ by honor and dishonor, by <u>evil report</u> and *good report; as <u>deceivers</u>, and yet true;* [9] *as unknown, and yet well known; as <u>dying</u>, and behold we live; as <u>chastened</u>, and yet not killed;* [10] *as <u>sorrowful</u>, yet always rejoicing; as <u>poor</u>, yet making many rich; as having <u>nothing</u>, and yet possessing all things.*

2 Corinthians 6-3-10 (underline added)

Actually, it gets worse. In 2 Corinthians 11, Paul writes:

Are they Hebrews? So am I. Are they Israelites? So am I. Are they the seed of Abraham? So am I. [23] *Are they ministers of Christ?—I speak as a fool—I am more: in <u>labors</u> more abundant, in <u>stripes</u> above measure, in <u>prisons</u> more frequently, in <u>deaths</u> often.* [24] *From the Jews five times I <u>received forty stripes minus one</u>.* [25] *Three times I was <u>beaten with rods</u>; once I was <u>stoned</u>; three times I was <u>shipwrecked</u>; a night and a day I have been in the <u>deep</u>;* [26] *in <u>journeys</u> often, in <u>perils</u> of waters, in <u>perils of robbers</u>, in <u>perils of my own countrymen</u>, in <u>perils of the Gentiles</u>, in <u>perils in the city</u>, in <u>perils in the wilderness</u>, in <u>perils in the sea</u>, in <u>perils among false brethren</u>;* [27] *in <u>weariness and toil</u>, in <u>sleeplessness often</u>, in <u>hunger and thirst</u>, in <u>fasting's often</u>, in <u>cold and nakedness</u>—* [28] *besides the other things, what comes upon me daily: my deep concern for all the churches.* [29] *Who is weak, and I am not weak? Who is made to stumble, and I do not burn with indignation?*

II Corinthians 11:22-29

Pursue Good and Not Evil

I am reminded of a story when Paul and Silas were beaten and put in prison for preaching the gospel. Instead of calling a lawyer to get them out of jail, they began to praise and worship God who in turn, caused an earthquake and allowed them to walk out of jail. But not before leading the jailer in a prayer of salvation. They were so consumed with doing the will of God that their beating and imprisonment were an opportunity to praise Jesus instead of being offended and seeking revenge. Most of the Christians I know (including myself) would probably stop preaching the first time they were stoned and left for dead, but Paul and Silas continued loving people and never repaid evil for evil.

Neil Anderson describes justice, mercy, and grace, and how we have been given these by God to extend to others:

> Consider these simple definitions of justice, mercy, and grace as they apply to relationships: justice is giving people what they deserve. If God were perfectly just in dealing with us we would all go to hell. God is a just God, and the wages of sin is death.
>
> Mercy is not giving people what they deserve. But when the kindness of God our Savior and his love for mankind appeared, he saved us, not on the basis of deeds which we have done in righteousness, but according to his mercy. Justice had to be served, so Jesus took upon himself the wrath of God.
>
> Grace is giving us what we don't deserve for by grace you have been saved through faith. Forgiveness and eternal life are free gifts from God. So the Lord instructs us to be merciful, just as your Father is merciful. We are not to give people what they

deserve; we are to give them what they don't deserve which is grace.

Neil Anderson

(Anderson, N. T. *Restored: Experience Life With Jesus*. Franklin, TN. e3 Resource, 2007)

When we think of getting beaten with rods, stoned and left for dead, or whipped five different times just as Paul was, it can be overwhelming. Normally, this kind of mistreatment rarely happens in our society. However, the temptation to repay evil for evil comes through other avenues: abuse in our marriages, family lives, jobs, churches, or our internal warped perspective.

Let me give you some examples from my personal life of when I acted out of pride and arrogance, repaying evil for evil instead of seeking the good in others. Note also how my regrettable actions affected my relationships in those areas.

Years ago, I was managing a gun store in Portland, Oregon. We had a great store and enjoyed selling firearms. Then the owner, along with one of my friends, thought it would be a good idea to add a fly fishing section to the store. The rest of the employees all felt it was a terrible idea and a huge waste of money. So being a natural team leader, I organized the complaints about the new idea and spearheaded the resistance. I realize there was no evil being done against me personally, but I certainly repaid evil for a decision I didn't agree with. When I look back on this situation, I know I was a terrible example as a Christian man and an even worse example as a staff pastor in a church. I needled and complained for months to John, the employee who helped the owner install the fly shop. It finally reached the point where I was sinning against John, the shop owner, and God. I was being evil to others and had to repent for the sin. But even worse, I caused a rift in all three relationships. As the manager of the store, I should have voiced my opinion and then dealt with the decision in a godly manner. I could have found the good in the situation and encouraged John and the owner in their endeavor. I clearly wasn't acting in godly character at the time. If I had, I would have looked a lot more like Jesus in thought, speech, and actions. Instead, I caused chasms in my relationships and I was a bad example of Jesus.

I hate to admit it, but over my 28+ years married to an awesome woman, I have repaid evil for evil far too many times. I would also venture a guess, based on my gun shop experience, that most of the time, no real evil was done towards me. The evil was the condition of my heart. Therefore, I reacted to something from a wrong perspective. Sure, there were times when Lori did the same, but instead of loving her and finding the good in the situation, I reacted with evil intent that only made things worse. I know that if I practiced the "one another's" from the beginning of my marriage in 1989, there would have been far fewer unwanted arguments. These "one another's" would have caused me to deal with my own hurts and insecurities, and enabled me to focus on living love with Lori.

As I write this, I can think of many times when people huddled around Jesus, asking Him questions to trick Him. Clearly, many people hated Jesus' message, but time after time, Jesus answered with love and compassion. He refused to be offended by people's evil motives. Had I been in the same situation, there would have been a fist fight because my competitive spirit would have arisen and taken charge.

While in my 30's and on staff at City Harvest Church, I sat in many elder's meetings trying to tame my competitive nature and not respond too aggressively to imagined slights or power plays. I don't know why, but if I thought one of the elders was acting out of arrogance or pride, I was ready to put him or her in their place. Clearly, the Lord needed to work in my heart so I wouldn't respond with wrong motives. Thank God, I have a great leadership team today at Living Stone Church of Spokane. We are able to discuss difficult issues affecting the church without me reacting negatively.

The one good thing I had going for me was that I knew down deep that I never had a good reason to repay evil for evil. I knew there was a root of bitterness driving my competition and that God had to root it out. I also knew I had to continually give my issues to God and submit to His word which transformed me. As I look back to 1987 when God called me to be a pastor in Spokane, WA, I now know why God didn't allow me to be a lead pastor until I was 42 years old; I needed a lot of healing in my life. Besides, God loves elders. If I would have pushed the issue and planted a church in my 30's, I would have offended and hurt a lot of people because of my competitive spirit. I loved people and I wanted them to have a relationship with Jesus, but I would have reacted out of pain and caused more offense in people's lives. Fortunately, Jesus has been working in me since 1987, getting me to think like Him, speak like Him, and act like Him.

Peter shows us how to respond to evil.

> *But how is it to your credit if you receive a beating for doing wrong and endure it? But if you suffer for doing good and you endure it, this is commendable before God. To this you were called, because Christ suffered for you, leaving you an example, that you*

should follow in his steps. "He committed no sin, and no deceit was found in his mouth." When they hurled their insults at Him, he did not retaliate; when he suffered, he made no threats. Instead, he entrusted himself to Him who judges justly.

1 Peter 2:20- 23

God's goal for every one of His followers is to act like Christ and not repay evil for evil, but instead pursue the good in others and bless them even if they are being evil against us. It sounds hard, but if we seek the grace and love of Jesus, He will help us act like Him in every situation.

APPLICATION

Let's think about this for a moment. Paul writes in Acts 24 that he was without offense towards men and God. How remarkable, considering it was men who did all these evil things to him. Further, it was God who allowed it all to happen. In fact, the Bible says that God told Paul he would suffer a lot for Jesus.

There must be something supernatural about Paul's life that allowed him to be so hurt and abused by others with no adverse effect on his mission. Eventually, Paul went on to Rome knowing that he would be beheaded for the gospel of Jesus Christ but joyful to be sharing the gospel.

As we consider the need to be cleansed and freed of all offense, hatred, and bitterness, let's not miss the severity of the condition. The person who believes it is all right to keep bitterness or unforgiveness in his or her life is living in rebellion towards God and is in danger of hell fire. I realize this is the most severe of examples, but we need to understand the direction in which we are trending when we harbor such evil in our hearts. In Matthew 18, Jesus taught that unless we forgive others as He forgave us, we are not going to escape damnation. It is important to fully appreciate the ramifications of that warning.

> *For if you forgive other people when they sin against you, your heavenly Father will also forgive you. But if you do not forgive others their sins, your Father will not forgive your sins.*
>
> Matthew 6:14-15

SELF EVALUATION OR GROUP DISCUSSION

- Why do you think we each have an internal tendency to repay evil with evil?

  o What does this tendency tell us about ourselves?

- Does repaying evil with good offend your sense of Justice? Why or why not?

- Imagine for a second that you were at a neighborhood block party and you had an opportunity to share about Jesus with one of your neighbors. Suddenly, in front of dozens of people, this person you were sharing with became enraged, began cursing you and punched you in the face. How would you respond, lying on the ground?

  o Would you fight back?

  o Would you yell and curse back as you ran off declaring that you are going to sue that person?

  o Is it possible that you could get up, shake the dust off your feet, and walk off unoffended because that is what Jesus asks us to do?

Pursue Good and Not Evil

- What if you were at school sharing with friends how you met Christ. Then someone came up making a huge scene about how you are a religious idiot and that you should stop talking about God.

  o Because you are around your peers and friends, would you feel humiliated and hurt? How would you respond?

  o Would you want to seek revenge, or is your relationship with Jesus so amazing that nothing offends you?

Make sure that nobody pays back wrong for wrong, but always strive to do what is good for each other and for everyone else.

1 Thessalonians 5:15

Do not repay anyone evil for evil. Be careful to do what is right in the eyes of everyone. [18] If it is possible, as far as it depends on you, live at peace with everyone. [19] Do not take revenge, my dear friends, but leave room for God's wrath, for it is written: "It is mine to avenge; I will repay," says the Lord. [20] On the contrary: "If your enemy is hungry, feed him; if he is thirsty, give him something to drink. In doing this, you will heap burning coals on his head." [21] Do not be overcome by evil, but overcome evil with good.

Romans 12:17-21

- Paul says to *seek to do good.* Why do we need to look for and pursue good? How is this different than passively waiting for the opportunity to come up?

- In what situations at home, at school, or at work is it most difficult for you to pursue the good of others? Why?

- Who offends or gets under your skin the most? Be candid.

- Do you think you have the potential to do good to them rather than stay mad?

- In Romans 12:17-21 (above), what does it mean to *leave room for God's wrath*?

- Why is it better to let God deal with evil than to try and deal with it yourself?

Finally, all of you, be like-minded, be sympathetic, love one another, be compassionate and humble. ⁹ Do not repay evil with evil or insult with insult. On the contrary, repay evil with blessing, because to this you were called so that you may inherit a blessing. ¹⁰ For, "Whoever would love life and see good days must keep their tongue from evil and their lips from deceitful speech. ¹¹ They must turn from evil and do good; they must seek peace and pursue it.

1 Peter 3:8-11

- What blessing do we receive for pursuing the good of others? What would happen at church if every member made a daily, conscious choice to pursue the good of others?

- Peter wrote about keeping our tongues from evil. Most of us never seek physical vengeance. Instead, we hold onto our anger and verbal venom. Are you holding grudges and remaining bitter towards those who hurt you? Are you repaying evil for evil? Explain.

- If you have a clear offense with someone, when should you talk to them about it? Sooner or later? Why?

- Many people come to the church wounded by the world.

How can you be a support to these people for their good and God's glory?

- Are there currently any sin issues in your life that are causing you to repay evil for evil rather than seeking the good in others?

- How do you rate yourself on a scale of 1-5 in pursuing one another's good and not repaying evil for evil with family, friends, coworkers, and church family?

If you find yourself repaying evil for evil instead of pursuing the good of others, consider asking the Holy Spirit to reveal why you do that. Like Paul, we shouldn't let any offense get in the way of our prize—Jesus Himself. We seek a relationship with Jesus that is so real and strong that hurt, pain, offenses, difficulty and mocking our Christianity only strengthens that relationship. Evil in our heart towards others greatly affects our ability to do the will of the Father. Our passion is to be busy doing the Lord's work and not worrying about being offended by God or men. Paul envisioned the glory of Jesus and eternity in heaven, and nothing anyone could do affected his job as a Christian. He built the Christian church, wrote much of what became the New Testament, and brought the kingdom of God to multitudes, all through Living Love.

PRAYER

Father, I ask that if there is anything in me that wants to repay evil for evil rather than pursuing the good of others, that You reveal it, even concerning people I dislike or avoid. I ask You, Holy Spirit, to help me right now. Compare my heart to the scriptures listed in this chapter. If I am easily hurt and offended, then my heart needs a transformation so I can look and act more like Jesus. Lord, when I think of certain people in my life or from my past, I feel hatred towards them and don't want to be around them. That hatred has affected my life for the worse in so many ways. Jesus, help me forgive others and live a life that is devoted to You so the people that hurt me don't affect my doing Your will. Amen.

****

Father, in Jesus name, I come directly to You with an honest heart. I have hatred, bitterness, and unforgiveness in my heart. I have kept this hidden for a long time and need Your help to uproot it. I have been offended by people who have hurt me. I have been offended in deep personal relationships and I can't seem to get rid of it. Jesus, I need help in giving this to You—please help me. I repent of my rebellious spirit and I come clean. Jesus, please forgive me of my rebellion. I admit that rebellion is knowingly going against Your word and commandments while still thinking I can still follow You. I know it is wrong to keep this inside but I have told myself that I don't care what You think Jesus. But now, I give You my rebellion and ask for Your love, mercy, forgiveness, and grace to flood my soul. Amen

JOURNAL

This is a great time to list things in your life that affect your relationship with Jesus and prevent you from doing His will. If you are offended and hurt from past events or people, know that Jesus can heal every last wound. If you were wronged, abused, mistreated or demeaned, this is a great time to forgive. Remember: The only one being hurt is you.

Go back and read through the opening scriptures describing what the Apostle Paul endured, and keep in mind that if Jesus could fill him with the Spirit in such a way that he forgave all who hurt him then Jesus will give you that same Spirit to heal all your wounds.

Write down what Jesus is showing and telling you through the Holy Spirit and His word. This might be an area where you need to pray with someone; if so, please seek out a church leader to help you. But remember, because of what Jesus did on the cross, you have 100% access to the Father in heaven.

NOTES

Live Love

6

Care, Encourage, and Help

Jesus walked through cities and countryside helping people who were weak and in need. I love the story of Jesus sailing across a lake and meeting a severely demon-possessed man who ran towards him. Although this man was so tormented that he had to live alone in the mountain country, there was something amazing about Jesus that attracted the man. Even the demons could not stop him from running to the Son of God. Jesus knew that this man would be in this condition for the rest of his life unless He intervened. In His love and compassion, Jesus spent time with him and then cast out the demons. The man was helpless until Jesus set him free.

It is interesting that Jesus spent so much of His time helping those who were possessed by demons. Demon possessed people aren't normally the people that the modern-day church helps, but Jesus loved to set people free from bondage. Consider His declaration from Isaiah, as recorded in Luke 4. Jesus had just returned from a 40 day fast during which He was tempted by Satan in the wilderness.

> *16 He went to Nazareth, where he had been brought up, and on the Sabbath day he went into the synagogue, as was his custom. He stood up to read, 17 and the*

scroll of the prophet Isaiah was handed to him. Unrolling it, he found the place where it is written:

The Spirit of the Lord is upon Me, because He anointed Me to preach the gospel to the poor. He has sent Me to proclaim freedom to the captives, and recovery of sight to the blind, to set free those who are oppressed, to proclaim the favorable year of the Lord.

Luke 4:16-19

Look at what Jesus proclaimed He was empowered to do:

- Preach the good news of salvation to the poor.
- Set people free who are held captive (including by demonic forces).
- Heal the blind, the sick, and the lame.
- Set people free from oppression (including depression).

Jesus is clearly the author of the original Live Love book because He had great compassion on those who were weak and in need.

Another story I love about Jesus is when He spent time with a Samaritan woman at a well, in John 4. While the disciples were gone getting food, Jesus began a conversation with a woman drawing her daily water. Jesus, in His love and compassion for weak and needy people, knew she had been married and divorced five times, and that she was currently living with a man to whom she wasn't married.

What makes her interaction with Jesus unique is that if a religious leader had heard her story, he would have condemned her and walked away. But Jesus was on a mission to care for the weak. Unlike many in His ministry, this woman did not need physical healing, but Jesus knew the condition of her heart, so He spent the time necessary for her to realize her desperate need for salvation. Jesus, in His love for souls, set her free from her captive state of sin and shame and was able to show her that she could live free from sin and death.

> *¹⁰ Jesus answered her, "If you knew the gift of God and who it is that asks you for a drink, you would have asked him and he would have given you living water."*

> *¹¹ "Sir," the woman said, "you have nothing to draw with and the well is deep. Where can you get this living water? ¹² Are you greater than our father Jacob, who gave us the well and drank from it himself, as did also his sons and his livestock?"*

> *¹³ Jesus answered, "Everyone who drinks this water will be thirsty again, ¹⁴ but whoever drinks the water I give them will never thirst. Indeed, the water I give them will become in them a spring of water welling up to eternal life."*

> *¹⁵ The woman said to him, "Sir, give me this water so that I won't get thirsty and have to keep coming here to draw water."*

John 4:10-15

Continuing her encounter with Jesus, the woman was convicted of her sin, but she never felt condemned by Jesus because His love toward her was so overwhelming. Jesus' heart was to bless and save, not to judge and condemn. Indeed, this is one of the few instances where He revealed who He truly was.

> *¹⁶ He told her, "Go, call your husband and come back."*

17 "I have no husband," she replied.

Jesus said to her, "You are right when you say you have no husband. 18 The fact is, you have had five husbands, and the man you now have is not your husband. What you have just said is quite true."

19 "Sir," the woman said, "I can see that you are a prophet.20 Our ancestors worshiped on this mountain, but you Jews claim that the place where we must worship is in Jerusalem."

21 "Woman," Jesus replied, "believe me, a time is coming when you will worship the Father neither on this mountain nor in Jerusalem. 22 You Samaritans worship what you do not know; we worship what we do know, for salvation is from the Jews. 23 Yet a time is coming and has now come when the true worshipers will worship the Father in the Spirit and in truth, for they are the kind of worshipers the Father seeks. 24 God is spirit, and his worshipers must worship in the Spirit and in truth."

25 The woman said, "I know that Messiah" (called Christ) "is coming. When he comes, he will explain everything to us."

26 Then Jesus declared, "I, the one speaking to you—I am he."

John 4:16-26

Jesus gave us the same power and love to help and care for the needy. All we need to do is choose to seek out people who need salvation, or set free from oppression, or healed from sickness.

Care, Encourage, and Help

Hold them in the highest regard in love because of their work. Live in peace with each other. And we urge you, brothers and sisters, warn those who are idle and disruptive, encourage the disheartened, help the weak, be patient with everyone.

1 Thessalonians 5:13-14

Going back to the scripture in Luke 4, the same calling that Jesus received to preach to, release, and heal people is what we receive when He anoints and fills us with His Spirit. He was reading that passage in Isaiah for Himself and for us.

AMANDA

So what does care, encourage, and help look like? Here is Amadan's story to illustrate these qualities.

Hi. My name is Amanda.

God put it on my heart a while back to tell people openly about my life, about the hurt I went through, how I got saved, and how salvation changed my life. I allowed people to know some things, but not everything, because I was scared. I thought they'd look at me and think: What a freak. What a loser. Why does she have to come here? Don't talk to her. She is too damaged. We can't save her. On top of it all, I thought: Why tell anyone about my life, because no one will listen. No one wants to here about how I got hurt in the past. They don't care about me, even though I was completely broken.

From what I remember, our parents were not in my life. My father would show up occasionally but I don't remember much about him. I thought that if I listened to my grandma and grandpa really well, maybe mom and dad would come back. But that did not happen, so I tried to make grandma and grandpa very happy, hoping that I would not lose them too. I would be happy when they got me stuff even though I didn't like it. It worked for years, and then out of nowhere, I was betrayed—abused by a man I trusted. Suddenly, the family I had was ripped away. After that, I found my sisters when I was living with our father, which was good. Then my sisters were never home, so it was OK until home was ripped away again. After that, I found myself living with my mother and stepfather and once again, it seemed good. I was in high school and life was starting to look like it was going to be all right. Then I came home from school one day and my mom was doing drugs. My life was ripped from me again. I thought that I was not wanted. Because I went through four different types of homes and four different families, I thought there was something wrong with me. Maybe it was all my fault. Maybe I was not good enough to deserve a family.

I wanted something of my own so I found a boyfriend. We had a daughter. He was not the best for me but I did not want him to leave me, so I stuck it out. And again, a family was ripped away from me. So I tried again and again and it just kept failing. All I wanted was a family to belong to, to love and be loved, to be happy with. In the back of my mind, I felt like no one wanted me, that I was a burden and stuck with the life I had. My life just kept getting harder. After a while, I got tired and screamed at God for all that I thought He allowed to happen in my life. I was so angry. I reached the point of wanting it all to end... one way or another.

Then my sister Michelle asked if I wanted to go to church. I said yes; I don't know why but I said yes. She took me to City Life Church (now Living Stone Church) and for the first time in a long time, I felt genuinely loved. I could not get enough of it. No one wanted anything in return, they just loved on me. It was as if they were giving away free love. I finally felt like I was wanted. I was so happy, I started to cry. At the end of the service, I immediately had a few ladies surrounded me and pray for me. This is when I knew that I belonged there, and that Jesus was in my heart. I went through a recovery program to help me with my past, and I had the help of Pastor Van and a book written by Neil Anderson called Restored. Reading through the book was painful and difficult. I lost track of how many times I threw it against the wall. It's amazing how deep it took me and the things I had to walk through.

With the help of some great people at the church—Kari, Natalie, Cassie, Geoff, Nate, Eric, Danielle, Monique, Lori, Kim and so many more—I was able to begin receiving healing for my soul. They ether helped me with books to read, or sat with me in a car when it was raining. They helped take my girl to school. Sometimes they took me for coffee, invited us to Thanksgiving dinner, or ensured I got to woman's retreats. My sister picked me up every Sunday and took me to church. Afterward, she would take me out to eat and help me feel normal and loved.

With all the time that has passed, and all the phone calls and help, I realized that this was the real deal. I have a huge family! My salvation is Living Stone Church and Jesus.

Today, I have a loving husband who loves me even though I am still going through the healing process. I have a church that helps me with anything I need. I know where I belong. I know that no matter what, I am loved and accepted for who I am. Because of my salvation and connection with Living Stone Church, I no longer have an empty heart. I can enjoy life. I know who my true Father is. I know without a doubt that I don't have to be good enough. I don't have to work for it, and I will never feel unloved or unwanted again. If, for some reason, my life would be ripped away from me, there is always heaven, and I am OK with that.

APPLICATION

On the contrary, those parts of the body that seem to be weaker are indispensable, [23] and the parts that we think are less honorable we treat with special honor. And the parts that are unpresentable are treated

with special modesty, [24] while our presentable parts
need no special treatment. But God has put the body
together, giving greater honor to the parts that lacked
it, [25] so that there should be no division in the body,
but that its parts should have equal concern for each
other. [26] If one part suffers, every part suffers with it;
if one part is honored, every part rejoices with it.

1 Corinthians 12:22-25

This is one of the greatest love verses in all of scripture. Sadly, many church leaders focus on the cool and talented people, but Jesus focused on the broken and unpopular people that were in desperate need of Him. And then they became the cool people!

SELF-EVALUATION OR GROUP DISCUSSIONS

- As a follower of Jesus, do you seek out the weaker and less-honorable people to help them?

  o Explain how your heart feels toward these people.

- During the workweek, who could you care for, encourage, and show patience toward? Family, friends, coworkers, neighbors? Explain.

- Ask yourself who among your church family is disheartened? Who is weak?

  o What steps can you take over the next few weeks and months to love these brothers and sisters?

- So many of the gospel stories deal with Jesus helping and healing people. As a follower of Jesus, is your life marked by helping broken and hurting people? Explain.

- How is caring for and encouraging nonbelievers going to win them to Christ?

- What is happening in the spirit realm when you help and encourage non-believers?
  - Consider John 4, about the woman at the well and how the Holy Spirit worked with her.

- When someone in your family becomes sick or is walking through a hard time at work, how can you care for them?

- On a scale of 1-5, how would you rate yourself in caring for and encouraging the weak?

Consider again the words Jesus used to declare His ministry.

The Spirit of the Lord is upon Me,

Because He anointed Me to preach the gospel to the poor.

He has sent Me to proclaim release to the captives

And recovery of sight to the blind,

To set free those who are oppressed,

To proclaim the favorable year of the Lord.

Luke 4:18-19 (NASB)

This is a great time to pray this scripture over your life in two ways. One way is to pray that Jesus, through the power of the Holy Spirit, will give you His supernatural love and compassion towards people. Another way is to pray to receive His power to share the gospel and heal the sick. The heart of Jesus is to do the Father's will. Our hearts are to become like His.

JOURNAL

Journal what the Lord is doing in you right now when it comes to caring for the weak and wanting to help people. Write down your honest thoughts towards others so Jesus can encourage you or change you.

Consider the scripture in 2 Corinthians:

> *The weapons we fight with are not the weapons of the world. On the contrary, they have divine power to demolish strongholds. We demolish arguments and every pretension that sets itself up against the knowledge of God, and we take captive every thought to make it obedient to Christ. And we will be ready to punish every act of disobedience, once your obedience is complete.*

2 Corinthians 10:4-6

It is good for you to continue to go back to this section of scripture and learn to bring every wrong and sinful thought captive so all your thoughts obey Jesus.

PRAYER

Father, in Jesus name, I come to You hungry and broken. I want to obey You and do Your will. You said that whatever we pray in Your name would be done for us. I ask that You give me Your supernatural love and compassion for people, so when I see needy and hurt people, my heart cries out for their soul to be saved and healed. I also pray that You give me the power to share the good news of Your salvation. I ask for the power and compassion of the Holy Spirit to set captives free from sin, shame, and oppression. I receive right now the power to lay hands on the sick and lame and see them recover. I receive the power to open blind eyes and to proclaim the favor of the Lord over people's lives.

I ask You to forgive me of any racist thoughts I have towards people that I don't like. Sometimes we dislike others and we are not even aware of it, so I ask You, Holy Spirit, to dig out any wrong thoughts I have towards others. I ask that You help me love my enemies and those who have hurt me from my past. I receive right now a fresh forgiveness from Jesus so I can forgive others who have sinned against me.

NOTES

7

Bear One Another's Burdens

Five minutes on Facebook will reveal people who are broken, hurting, and needing someone to help them with their many burdens. Some people are engrossed in depression so deeply that they have no idea how to get out or where to look for help. For many, the burdens of their sins and addictions are a repetitive cycle of destruction for which they have no answer. Destructive lifestyles and learned behavior from their families cause many to give up. Because of the heavy burdens of sin and shame, many commit suicide, which in turn causes more destructive behavior for their friends and family.

To appreciate the work of God in the face of man's fallen condition, try to calculate the spiritual weight of your sin, shame, and every bad thought you have ever had. Then multiply that by 100 billion people over the last 7,000 years of human history, and then add 100 billion more people for the next several thousand years (assuming Jesus doesn't return first). How much spiritual weight do you think that is? The sin, shame, sickness, rebellion, and destruction for all humans over the last 7000 years is beyond our comprehension, but this is the amount of sin that Jesus took upon Himself so we can have a relationship with our Father for eternity.

The perfect sacrifice of Jesus Christ paid for all of humanity's sin: past, present, and future. Jesus is the ultimate burden bearer. He truly is the answer.

CHRIS AND CARRIE

Here is a short story of some great friends who started coming to our church three years ago and have blossomed into great servants for Jesus. Chris and Carrie had some burdens from past church experiences. I was able to walk with them and show that church is supposed to be fun and uplifting. I encouraged them to come in, plug in, and allow others to get to know them. I saw great gifts in Chris and Carrie and knew that they just needed time to heal and build some friendships within the church. They are now a part of our Ministry Coordinator Team that helps steer and provide vision for the church.

> We were brought to Living Stone Church by our youngest daughter. She made friends with another little 1st-grade girl in her school. They were soon best friends and we "had to go to her church!" I did not want to. My wife was then invited to a ladies' event by the girl's mom that September. Then by November, my wife had talked me, quite reluctantly, into bringing the whole family to the little white church building. When she had attended, she felt comfortable there simply because she wasn't the only person with tattoos and she didn't feel judged. "Happy wife" and all that.
>
> We hadn't been to church in a few years because we felt very used in our last church experience, which was my wife's first. I didn't want to go back to church again, that being the last of several negative

church experiences in my life. I knew God, but I didn't want anything to do with the church. Our family has no problem making friends on our own. We love to hang out and have fun with people, but there was something lacking in our life. We could still be Christians on our own without all the trouble of dealing with "church," but that attitude had led us down some pretty dark roads and we were hurting even more than when we had left the church years earlier.

From the first time I was invited by the pastor to a men's live love small group, I was expecting another religious club, but it was just some guys hanging out, eating bagels and talking about the word of God and their lives. Time went on and the patience and love of my pastor and many other people in our church proved that they just wanted to be our friends. I kept waiting for the catch, but there wasn't one. These were normal people with real lives and dealing with real issues by God's word.

Through God's word, I know that Jesus also lived love out in a way that was real. He met people right where they were. Jesus was unafraid to ask real questions about their lives. He also wanted to see them healed from their pain, injuries, and illnesses. I am learning how to share my own failings and pain with people, along with the triumphs—how to just give back out what Jesus has already given into me. Living love.

Chris and Carrie Murphy

Live Love

COME TOGETHER

Jesus commanded His followers to become ministers of reconciliation.

> *Come to me, all you who are weary and burdened, and I will give you rest.* [29] *Take my yoke upon you and learn from me, for I am gentle and humble in heart, and you will find rest for your souls.* [30] *For my yoke is easy and my burden is light."*

> Matthew 11:28-30

> *Therefore, we are ambassadors for Christ, as though God were making an appeal through us; we beg you on behalf of Christ, be reconciled to God.* [21] *He made Him who knew no sin to be sin on our behalf, so that we might become the righteousness of God in Him.*

> 2 Corinthians 5:20-21 (NASB)

Jesus spent three and a half years teaching His disciples to live love and bare one another's burdens. After Jesus left and was seated at the right hand of the Father, He gave us the ministry of reconciliation—restoring the relationship of man to God. He taught His disciples to preach salvation to the lost and set people free from their burdens through the power of the Holy Spirit. Our greatest calling as followers of Jesus is to bring people to the salvation knowledge of Jesus Christ and help restore their relationship to the Father as in the Garden of Eden.

BEARING BURDENS

There is a story in the Old Testament of the Israelites in a battle while Moses stood on a mountain looking down on the battlefield. God told Moses to raise his staff above his head. As long as his staff was above his head, the Israelites advanced in the battle. But when Moses got tired and dropped his staff, the Israelites would start losing. So Moses had two people stand at his side to help him keep his staff above his head.

Just as Moses needed help bearing the burden, so we need help from our fellow brothers and sisters in Christ to help bear our burdens to win the battle. God designed the church to help each other.

Now, bearing burdens doesn't mean that we take on their sin and shame—Jesus already did that. Rather, it means that we are so full of love for people that we help them bring their burdens to Jesus so they can be healed and restored. It means that we take the time to help people as we were helped. Godly mothers and fathers can teach their children to walk through the stresses of life. They also serve their children, teaching them to serve others. A servant is no lower than the person he serves. Instead, he puts others first, caring for them and helping them to bring their burdens to Jesus. Helping people with their burdens means walking with them until they are able to release their burdens to Jesus. It is walking with them until they walk in the Freedom of Christ.

Here is a great verse to help people confess their sins to Jesus and be set free from the weight of sin. Apply it to your own life, and share it with others who need Jesus.

> *How blessed is he whose transgression is forgiven, Whose sin is covered! How blessed is the man to whom the Lord does not impute iniquity, and in whose spirit there is no deceit! When I kept silent about my sin, my body wasted away through my groaning all day long. For day and night Your hand was heavy upon me; My vitality was drained away as with the*

fever heat of summer. Selah. I acknowledged my sin to You, and my iniquity I did not hide; I said, "I will confess my transgressions to the Lord"; and You forgave the guilt of my sin.

Psalms 32:1-5 (NASB)

APPLICATION

In the verse below, notice that God calls David a man after His heart. Yet, how can God say that when David committed some serious sins?

After He had removed Saul, He raised up David to be their king, concerning whom He also testified and said, 'I have found David the son of Jesse, a man after my own heart, who will do all My will.

Acts 13:22 (NASB)

First, it was no surprise to God that David committed some awful sins. We all do. But looking deeper into the life of David, we see a man who would do whatever God wanted him to do. David was more concerned about God's will than his own.

David loved and cared for people just as God does. By having this love for others, it captured the heart of God. We too are to have a heart to care for the burdens of others.

There is an illustration of this from when David became King of Israel.

When Mephibosheth son of Jonathan, the son of Saul, came to David, he bowed down to pay him honor. David said, "Mephibosheth!" "At your service," he replied. "Don't be afraid," David said to him, "for I will surely show you kindness for the sake of your father Jonathan. I will restore to you all the land that belonged to your grandfather Saul, and you will always eat at my table." [8] Mephibosheth bowed down and said, "What is your servant, that you should notice a dead dog like me?"

2 Samuel 9:6-8

What makes this a great story is that, unlike a new king who would have had the family of his predecessor killed so they wouldn't pose a challenge, David sought the relatives of Saul—the man who tried to kill him for 13 years—and restored to them any land that they owned when Saul was king. David not only restored land, he admitted Mephibosheth—a cripple—into his palace and let him eat at his (David's) own table. This is exactly what God does for us. Even though we were once enemies of God through our sinfulness, Jesus takes us in and lets us eat at His table.

Consider again the verses above. How does your heart align with them in caring for the burdens of others? Do you purpose in your heart to help burdened people? Jesus built His church from 12 people broken and conflicted with sin and hatred towards others. Along with these 12, He added tax collectors, adulterers, prostitutes, and many demon-possessed people to establish the New Testament church. Jesus accepted prideful and sexually immoral people carrying the burdens of unrighteousness and turned them into God-loving, God-fearing people. Today, He turns us around and anoints us to do what He did. True Christianity doesn't end when we get saved and healed of our burdens; it only begins. Christianity isn't just about our new relationship with Jesus; it is about us helping others find the same relationship with Jesus.

Live Love

Self Evaluation or Group Study Questions

Consider the following.

> *Brothers and sisters, if someone is caught in a sin, you who live by the Spirit should restore that person gently. But watch yourselves, or you also may be tempted. Carry each other's burdens, and in this way you will fulfill the law of Christ.*

> Galatians 6:1-2

> *Every high priest is selected from among the people and is appointed to represent the people in matters related to God, to offer gifts and sacrifices for sins. [2] He is able to deal gently with those who are ignorant and are going astray, since he himself is subject to weakness.*

> Hebrews 5:1-2

- If we are to carry each other's burdens, we first need to realize others have burdens. How can you be intentional in recognizing when someone around you is burdened?

- Why are we to be gentle with people as they bring their sins and burdens to Jesus?

- When have you had your burdens carried by another brother or sister in Christ?

  o How did this impact you?

- In what sense does bearing someone's burdens cost you something?

> *Therefore, if anyone is in Christ, the new creation has come: The old has gone, the new is here! All this*

is from God, who reconciled us to himself through Christ and gave us the ministry of reconciliation: that God was reconciling the world to himself in Christ, not counting people's sins against them. And he has committed to us the ministry of reconciliation.

2 Corinthians 5:17-19

As a prisoner for the Lord, then, I urge you to live a life worthy of the calling you have received. Be completely humble and gentle; be patient, bearing with one another in love. Make every effort to keep the unity of the Spirit through the bond of peace.

Ephesians 4:1-3

- What does it mean to say Christ has reconciled us to Himself?

- If Christ does not count our sins against us, why are we tempted to count the sins of others against them?

- What role does the Holy Spirit play in developing the character traits we see in Ephesians 4:1-3?

  o Pray through this list asking the Spirit to make these true in your life.

- What do we do if the person we are trying to help continues to refuse to bring their sin and burdens to Jesus?

- How would you rate yourself on a scale of 1-5 in the area of bearing the burdens of others?

JOURNAL

Write down your normal weekly schedule and ask the Holy Spirit if He wants you to adjust your schedule to be more focused on His will instead of your will. As a pastor, the greatest pleasure I get out of life is watching people grow in Christ and learn to give their burdens to Jesus. Jesus has called all Christians to help each other live lives free of sinful burdens. This starts with helping nonbelievers come to Christ, and it follows with helping our brothers and sisters. Let's pray and write down everything that the word and the Spirit are saying to us.

PRAYER

Father, in Jesus name, I submit to Your will of loving and caring for burdened people. Even though I mess up and don't always get it all right, I ask You to give me a passionate heart for the hurting, broken, and burdened people. Holy Spirit, I repent of my selfish desires to only look at my needs instead of the needs of others. Please flood my heart and life right now with Your power and love. Lord, I admit that my focus in life is more about myself and less about others. I am asking You to help me crucify those selfish parts of me so I can do Your will of caring for others. I also ask that You help me point people to You so they can be healed and released of their burdens. Amen.

NOTES

<u>Live Love</u>

8

Be Kind and Compassionate

When <Jesus> saw the crowds, he had compassion
on them, because they were harassed and helpless,
like sheep without a shepherd.

Matthew 9:36

Jesus could see both the outside and inside of people, and He knew when they were harassed and helpless. (Another translation says "distressed and dispirited.")

Can you see people the way Jesus sees them? You can if you look with the eyes of the Holy Spirit. The Holy Spirit has anointed and empowered all Christians to see, think, speak, and do what Jesus did. Obviously, we are not God, but as followers of Jesus, we have the Godhead living within us.

I said, 'You are "gods"; you are all sons of the Most
High.'"

Psalm 82:6

When Jesus and His disciples were surrounded by 10,000+ people eager for His teaching, He had compassion on them. He knew they were tired and hungry. The disciples didn't see things the same way. They said to send them away. But Jesus told His disciples to feed them. The disciples were completely flabbergasted and had no clue what to do. This is because they weren't looking at the people through eyes of compassion. They could only see through their own selfish lens. Instead of lost souls needing a savior, the disciples only saw a burden that they wanted Jesus to remove.

You might ask yourself what it really means to be kind and compassionate to one another—especially to strangers without Christ. The answers lie in this question: Do you ever find yourself weeping for lost people who don't know Christ? When you gaze at a group of people, do you wonder if they will spend an eternity in hell without Christ? If you answered "No" to these questions, then chances are you need to be infused with the compassion of Jesus Christ. Jesus came to save sinners from the wrath of God. He proved it by hanging on the cross and becoming the sacrificial Lamb of God.

Now, don't fall into condemnation. It is all right to admit that you have no concern for the lost. If you want it, however, Jesus will give you His compassion. The more you see lost people and have compassion on them, the more you turn your life's energy to the Father's will. God will meet you where you are. Jesus proved this when dealing with the faithlessness of a father whose son needed deliverance.

> *Immediately the boy's father exclaimed, "I do believe; help me overcome my unbelief!"*

> Mark 9:24

John the Baptist, when he saw Christ, stated: *"I must decrease while He must increase"* (John 3:30). John the Baptist not only saw the physical form of Jesus, he also saw the Lamb of God who would die for the sins of the world. John witnessed firsthand the salvation of sinners in the person of Jesus.

MY STORY

As much as I hate to admit this, kindness isn't something that comes naturally to me. I grew up learning to be tough. Making matters worse, I didn't have a father to teach me to love others. I ran with a lot of tough friends of my older brother and uncles who taught me how to kick and punch to do the most harm. Needless to say, I wasn't enrolled in the kindness class of love and comforting. When I played sports in high school, I tried to seriously hurt my opponents, even knock them out of the game if I could. I was big and fast for High School football, and I took every advantage available. I'd hit so hard, the other players either *couldn't* come back or *wouldn't* come back. My senior year at Inchelium High School, I knocked out an average of three people per game. Some left in ambulances, others limped away, but none returned. When I got to college to play football at Eastern Washington University (EWU) in Cheney, Washington, even though I was only an average player compared to the pool of talent there, I was still driven by a passion to hit people as hard as I could.

I recall a couple of specific plays from my senior year at EWU which proved my need for the kindness of the Lord. I had been a Christian for two years at this point—still learning a lot, still feeling scalding conviction when I did something terribly wrong.

At a game at Joe Albi Stadium, in the fall of 1989, I was running as fast as I could to catch up with a running back from the University of Montana. As I ran, I swore at him, hurling f-bombs and every other cuss word known to man. After the game, I sat in locker room wondering why all that junk came out of my mouth. I knew I needed help from God. It was more than curses that concerned me, however. It was the murderous rage at the heart of the curses.

Another play that season happened in Boise, Idaho, in the stadium with the blue field. It was the 4th quarter and I was trying to catch up to a tight end that had just caught a pass and was heading to the end zone. Just as I reached out to make the tackle, a Boise State wide receiver slammed his helmet into the side of my right knee. I lay on the field in so much pain, I thought my leg was broken. A couple of coaches ran out on the field with the trainer and eventually helped me off—a condition I usually inflicted on others. I was so infuriated at the dirty hit that when I reached the sidelines, I slammed my helmet into the ground. Seeing my outburst and wishing to show their sympathy for my misfortune, 24,000 Boise State fans started taunting me by calling out my number. As I limped to the benches, I responded by flipping off all 24,000 fans with both middle fingers. (Well, technically it was 12,000 per finger.) This act of brilliance was like tossing gas on a fire. The fans went crazy, yelling hysterically, hurling invectives, and mocking my injury. Where I was in agony and acting stupidly, they were thrilled with the opportunity I'd provided to taunt me.

On the six-hour bus ride home from Boise, I suffered intense conviction. What was inside me that caused me to flip off an entire stadium of football fans? (Thankfully, the equipment manager had forgotten my M16!) As a follower of Jesus, my actions certainly did not represent my Lord and His compassion for people. I knew I had a long way to go.

I share this to tell you that some of the things God demands from us are not easy or natural to our flesh. Some things are hard, requiring continuous work as we read and study the scriptures. Personally, I have to practice and pray through the scriptures on kindness to stay walking in the Spirit and not the flesh. In my years of walking with God, I've learned that between the power of the word of God and the Holy Spirit, there isn't anything in life that cannot be overcome with God's love and compassion. Even a stadium full of Boise State fans.

Self Evaluation Questions

- How would you rate yourself on a scale of 1-5 in the area of being kind and compassionate towards family, friends, coworkers, and your church family?

  Get rid of all bitterness, , brawling and slander, along with every form of malice. Be kind and compassionate to one another, forgiving each other, just as in Christ God forgave you.

  Ephesians 4:31-32

  Jesus replied: "'Love the Lord your God with all your heart and with all your soul and with all your mind.' This is the first and greatest commandment. And the second is like it: 'Love your neighbor as yourself.' All the Law and the Prophets hang on these two commandments."

  Matthew 22:37

- How is getting rid of bitterness and rage an active pursuit in the life of a Christian?

- In what situations in your life are you tempted to be bitter?

  o How can you fight against bitterness?

- How would your work environment change if you brought the spirit of kindness and compassion to work each day?

- Who at your school, church, or workplace do you find it really difficult to be kind and compassionate toward?

- After reading through this book and all the scriptures we are commanded to obey, has your heart been gradually changing towards people? Explain.

¹² Therefore, as God's chosen people, holy and dearly loved, clothe yourselves with compassion, kindness, humility, gentleness and patience. ¹³ Bear with each other and forgive one another if any of you has a grievance against someone. Forgive as the Lord forgave you. ¹⁴ And over all these virtues put on love, which binds them all together in perfect unity.

Colossians 3:12-14

- How does the first part of verse 12 describe the church?

- How does the last part say we should respond to that?

- What verb did Paul use in verse 12 to describe what Christians are supposed to do to have godly character?

  o Why is this a helpful word to use?

- Have you noticed a difference in your love towards people in the last few weeks since you have been reading this book?

- What spiritual disciplines and practices can you list that would help you become more kind and compassionate?

- What are some scriptures that you struggle with pertaining to the "one anothers" of this book?

- Is it easy and natural for you to care for people, build them up, and be an encourager?

- How easy is it to be kind and compassionate to people all the time?

Be Kind and Compassionate

JOURNAL

List the things that are more difficult for you to conquer and ask the Holy Spirit to help you in those areas. As you evaluate yourself and journal your thoughts on this, the Holy Spirit will empower you.

PRAYER

Father, being kind and compassionate isn't natural and easy for me. I really need Your help. Having compassion on lost people that always seem to sabotage their own lives through stupid decisions is hard for me. So I'm asking You to give me a new heart towards people that frustrate me. Jesus, You had compassion on everyone You met because You saw the condition of their soul and their need for salvation. As I sit here and ponder these scriptures, will You please flood me with Your compassion and love for people. I am asking for a fresh new in filling of the Holy Spirit and a capacity to love others as You do Jesus. Amen.

NOTES

9

Consider, Serve and Submit

Well done, good and faithful servant! You have been faithful with a few things; I will put you in charge of many things. Come and share your master's happiness!

Matthew 25:21

These are the words that I want to hear from Jesus after I die. I know we live in a "me first" culture, but that is not what Jesus taught us, nor is it what Jesus lived out. WWJD is an acronym for What Would Jesus Do. For years, Christians have had WWJD inscribed on their wristbands, T-shirts, and hats, but do we truly live out what Jesus lived out? His was a life of sacrifice and service. Is WWJD inscribed on our hearts?

From the time Jesus was baptized in the Jordan River at 30 years old, everything He did was to serve people and point them to the Father. Jesus was the God of the universe that created everything that we can see and touch, but He came as a servant to show people the way to heaven.

Jesus could have sat in the Jewish Temple and beckoned people to Him every day to hear His teachings. Instead, He chose to live among the people, visiting places that the religious leaders of Israel avoided. He walked the dusty roads where the blind beggars pleaded for money. He frequented the forbidden areas where lepers cried "Unclean!" But instead of fleeing them, he healed them. He stayed with sinners and listened to their stories as He loved and forgave them. He gathered tax collectors like Matthew and Zacchaeus, forgiving their sins and making them faithful servants in His Kingdom. Jesus cared for adulterous and demon-possessed women, restoring their souls and enlisting them in the Kingdom of God.

The life of Jesus was one of power and authority in the service of others. He made them more important than Himself. Even though Jesus was equal with the Father, He made Himself subject to the Father and lived a life in complete submission to the Father's will. The Father's will was to restore people to Him, and the only way to do that was to send His Son to be a sacrifice for the world. Jesus became the Lamb slain for the sins of the world.

CASSIE AND GEOFF

Here is a short testimony from a wonderful couple that Lori and I have helped grow into a powerful couple for Jesus. Geoff and Cassie Morgan are a great strength in our church and good friends to us. Ministry is all about making people more important than yourselves and watching them grow in maturity, following Jesus with all their hearts.

> We were living separate lives. Cassie was a young adult small group leader and was very connected to her church and saw them as her God-given family. I (Geoff) was living for myself and needed to get my life refocused on God and all He had for me. She was living with a family from her church and I was

sleeping on my cousin's couch. I began attending City Harvest Church in Vancouver, WA in January 2003 and met Cassie through a mutual friend. When I decided I wanted to marry Cassie, I met the couple she was living with and quickly realized they would be a vital part of our lives forever. They became our accountability partners, facilitated our premarital counseling, threw us a baby shower, and have walked through all the seasons of our marriage with us. Fourteen years later and we are still walking out life together at Living Stone Church in Spokane, WA with the same couple. God opened their hearts to us and we have grown not only individually but as a couple and family with our two kids—Reliance and Ezekiel. We have walked out our faith with them living love and being loved."

WORK WELL

In America, we are taught that if you work hard you can get ahead in life. While there is some truth to this—hard work is a godly characteristic—"work hard" can mean "walk over" as we learn to use people to get ahead in life. Unlike the pyramid of capitalism, the kingdom of God is an upside down kingdom. It is a place where God gives out rewards and blessings based on service to Him and others, submitting to and honoring each other in love. In the end, we can only enter into God's heavenly eternity if we are faithful servants who submit to the Father's will.

> *"Not everyone who says to me, 'Lord, Lord,' will enter the kingdom of heaven, but only the one who does the will of my Father who is in heaven.*

Matthew 7:21

109

There is nothing wrong with making money and being successful in life, but our lives are to reflect the life of Christ as servants to our fellow man.

MY STORY

In the 90's, I worked in retail in the Sporting Goods Hunting and Firearms industry. We had a few departments requiring knowledgeable salespeople. For example, there was ammo reloading, handgun personal defense, ammunition, long distance target shooting, high-end rifle and optics for hunting, and many other sub-categories. I was blessed to manage two different stores for about nine years. Fortunately, I had a knowledgeable crew in each store. As a manager and follower of Jesus, it was my goal to serve each employee, helping them do their best in their specialized area. This required that I lay down my pride and serve them above my own ambitions. I knew each area of the store well but I looked for people who knew more than I did so we could have the best stores in Portland.

During my time as manager, we had a lot of competition and knew many of the other stores' employees. As I got to know other managers, I saw that they managed people out of a position of power and control instead of serving their coworkers and trying to set a personal example of servant leadership. Because these managers lorded over their employees, it made a huge difference in the way the employees acted and talked about them. Not surprisingly, the employees were always seeking to come and work for us because of our positive environment. I certainly wasn't perfect in the way I managed, and I also had to deal with my own selfishness and pride issues, but the employees respected me and I respected them. Above all, I wanted to be a godly example to the people I managed so they would eventually come to Christ. I had an important position as a manager over people but my end goal as a follower of Jesus was to see people come to Christ. And it must have worked because a few actually became followers of Jesus and started attending church. As I look back on these years of managing people, it taught me a lot about being a pastor and loving people above myself.

OTHERS FIRST

Jesus knows we are not perfect in the sense of being sinless. Yet, He requires His followers to be servants. As representatives of His love, we are to put others before us. As we do this, Jesus supports us. It's hard for some people to serve and put other first because they wrestle with jealousy, pride, trust, and selfish ambitions. But when we obey God's word and put others first, God blesses us with a deeper relationship with Him. Everything else in our lives flows from that blessing: better jobs, better relationships, a guilt-free conscience, and the enjoyment of material wealth.

I like to relate "serving others" to our tithes and offerings. Scripture says when we give to God, He pours out a blessing from heaven and rebukes the devourer for us.

> *I will prevent pests from devouring your crops, and the vines in your fields will not drop their fruit before it is ripe," says the Lord Almighty.*

> Malachi 3:11

As we give to God, we are actually saying: "God, I trust and worship you with everything I have." In the same way, when we put others first, trying our best to bless them, God pours out a blessing on us. What we are actually saying to God is: "God, as I serve others, I am trying to show them who you are. In doing so, I know that you will promote me and bless me." As we apply this principle to our occupations, we find that instead of trying to climb the corporate ladder through competition, we get to the top through serving others, being honest, and working hard. Jesus sees every step we take. He hears our every thought. So learn to rest in Jesus, serve others, and Jesus will have your back and take care of you.

Putting others first in all areas of our lives allows people to see Jesus' love and compassion for them. As they observe our servant's hearts, the Holy Spirit will work in their hearts to show them Jesus working through us. Let's face it. Having someone truly serve others to build them up and encourage them is unusual. Therefore, when we, as true Christians, lay down our fleshly ambitions and truly serve others, they are going to wonder why. I have been asked dozens of times over the years why I serve others as I do. This gives me an opportunity to share Christ with them. The cool thing is, they have already seen me work hard and serve, so they cannot deny something is different about me. They have seen Jesus at work in me and have begun to trust me. In truth, they are trusting Jesus in me, but they don't always know that…at least, not at first.

APPLICATION

I encourage you to spend a day or more fasting, praying, and asking God to give you a new and inspired revelation of Jesus being both God in heaven and mankind's servant on earth. It takes a revelation from the Holy Spirit to begin understanding the true love that God has for people—a love to make Him come as a servant and hang on a cross for us.

SELF EVALUATION OR GROUP STUDY QUESTIONS

Do nothing out of selfish ambition or vain conceit. Rather, in humility value others above yourselves, ⁴ not looking to your own interests but each of you to the interests of the others.

Philippians 2:3-4

Above all, love each other deeply, because love covers over a multitude of sins. [9] Offer hospitality to one another without grumbling. [10] Each of you should use whatever gift you have received to serve others, as faithful stewards of God's grace in its various forms. [11] If anyone speaks, they should do so as one who speaks the very words of God. If anyone serves, they should do so with the strength God provides, so that in all things God may be praised through Jesus Christ. To Him be the glory and the power forever and ever. Amen.

1 Peter 4:8-11

Love must be sincere. Hate what is evil; cling to what is good. [10] Be devoted to one another in love. Honor one another above yourselves.

Romans 12:9-10

- How would you define *humility* and *honor*?

- If we are to value the interests of others, we have to first know what their interests are. What helps us understand what is going on in someone's life?

- How could you take a special interest in someone's life at school or work?

- How well do you honor above yourself the people you are in regular contact with? Explain.

When the ten heard about this, they were indignant with the two brothers. [25] Jesus called them together and said, "You know that the rulers of the Gentiles lord it over them, and their high officials exercise authority over them. [26] Not so with you. Instead, whoever wants to become great among you must be your servant, [27] and

113

whoever wants to be first must be your slave—²⁸ just as the Son of Man did not come to be served, but to serve, and to give his life as a ransom for many."

Matthew 20:24-28

Always give thanks to God the Father for everything, in the name of our Lord Jesus Christ. ²¹ Submit to one another out of reverence for Christ.

Ephesians 5:20-21

- Is there anything particularly challenging about Jesus' words in Matthew?

- Why did Jesus say He came?

- What situation was Jesus responding to in these verses in Matthew?

- Do you identify more with Christ or the disciples?

- If you want to be great in God's economy, you have to be a servant. If you want to be first, then you must be last. What does it look like to be a servant in every area of your life?

- How do we model Christ when we submit to other people? Pray for an opportunity to serve someone at home, work or school this week with the goal of showing them Christ.

- Do you ever feel like others are ignoring you or trying to distance themselves from you? If so, why?

- How would you rate yourself on a scale of 1-5 in the area of considering others more important yourself and serving others?

PRAYER/JOURNAL

At this point, I ask you to come up with your own prayer as you seek God in the areas we've discussed. Maybe you have a hard time keeping a job or getting promotions at work. Maybe you always find yourself butting heads with coworkers or your boss and wonder why you never get ahead. Maybe you have a hard time connecting with people like family and friends or coworkers. Maybe you talk too much and don't listen well.

I encourage you to write out your prayer based on the scriptures above, considering how you line up with them. Also, write out what you feel the Holy Spirit is saying to you about serving and honoring others above yourself and helping people with their interests above your own.

Live Love

NOTES

10

Forgiveness and Harmony

God is good! For God to send His Son to die on a cross as the sacrificial lamb for my sin is indescribable, unfathomable, unexplainable, and unimaginable. My sin has been atoned for and washed away by the perfect blood of Jesus Christ.

> All forgiveness is substitutionary. Christ paid the price for our sins, and we pay the price for those who sin against us. In a practical sense, forgiveness is agreeing to live with the consequences of another person sins. "But that isn't fair," some protest. Of course it isn't, but we will have to do it anyway. Everybody is living with the consequences of somebody else's sin. We are all living with the consequences of Adam's sin. We have the choice to live in the bondage of bitterness or in the freedom of forgiveness.
>
> Neil Anderson

(Anderson, N. T. *Restored: Experience Life With Jesus*. Franklin, TN. e3 Resource, 2007)

When the nation of Israel was enslaved in Egypt, God sent Moses to deliver them from the bondage of slavery. In the process, God inflicted His famous ten plagues on Egypt to show that He was God. The Egyptians learned quickly that He backed up what He said, and that they needed to release the Jews from bondage or else. For the 10th plague, God sent His death angel to kill the firstborn in every household in Egypt, which included both the Jews and Egyptians. However, God instructed Moses to have the Jews kill a lamb and put its blood on the doorposts of each house. When the death angel came to that house and witnessed the blood, it passed over that house and went to the next house. Thus the Jews were spared while the firstborn of the Egyptians were killed.

In New Testament terms, Jesus was that slain Lamb whose blood covers the doorposts of your life. As a believer, when the wrath of God comes in judgment, He will pass over your life because God sees the perfect and spotless blood of Jesus on your life. Jesus has forgiven your sin because you have accepted His sacrifice for sin. This is the greatest miracle in history. Man lacked a way to the Father but Jesus came and bridged that impassable chasm between the Father and us. Our offense against God was so wide and deep that there was no way for any human to reach God, but Jesus did it.

The story below from Matthew 18 illustrates this.

> *21 Then Peter came to Jesus and asked, "Lord, how many times shall I forgive my brother or sister who sins against me? Up to seven times?"*
>
> *22 Jesus answered, "I tell you, not seven times, but seventy-seven times.*
>
> *23 "Therefore, the kingdom of heaven is like a king who wanted to settle accounts with his servants. 24 As he began the settlement, a man who owed him ten*

thousand bags of gold was brought to him. ²⁵ Since he was not able to pay, the master ordered that he and his wife and his children and all that he had be sold to repay the debt.

²⁶ *"At this the servant fell on his knees before him. 'Be patient with me,' he begged, 'and I will pay back everything.' ²⁷ The servant's master took pity on him, canceled the debt and let him go.*

²⁸ *"But when that servant went out, he found one of his fellow servants who owed him a hundred silver coins. He grabbed him and began to choke him. 'Pay back what you owe me!' he demanded.*

²⁹ *"His fellow servant fell to his knees and begged him, 'Be patient with me, and I will pay it back.'*

³⁰ *"But he refused. Instead, he went off and had the man thrown into prison until he could pay the debt. ³¹ When the other servants saw what had happened, they were outraged and went and told their master everything that had happened.*

³² *"Then the master called the servant in. 'You wicked servant,' he said, 'I canceled all that debt of yours because you begged me to. ³³ Shouldn't you have had mercy on your fellow servant just as I had on you?' ³⁴ In anger his master handed him over to the jailers to be tortured, until he should pay back all he owed.*

³⁵ *"This is how my heavenly Father will treat each of you unless you forgive your brother or sister from your heart."*

Matthew 18:21-35

FORGIVENESS

Some people have been so hurt by others that they feel it is impossible to forgive even though they themselves have received complete forgiveness from God. This is painful for some to understand, but if we take the absolute worst possible things that have been done against people, it can't compare to our sin against a Holy and Perfect God. Murder, rape, sexual or physical abuse—none of those sins can compare to our sin against a holy God.

Jesus used the analogy of financial debt to say that the worst possible sin against you by someone else is equivalent to one bag of silver. Yet, the sin that we have done against God is 10,000 bags of gold—impossible to repay. The moral of Jesus' story is this: If I (Jesus) have come and forgiven your sin against Me, then forgiving others, no matter how ugly the offense, is not optional. It is a requirement. As hard as this is to hear, the reason we struggle with this is that we are selfish. We want to hold grudges. Ultimately, we want to be the judge that repays the person who hurt us.

The problem with this line of thought is that we are not perfect as Jesus is, so we are incapable of properly judging others. Only God can correctly judge the sins of others.

HARMONY

Forgiveness and submission are keys to living in harmony with each other. As discussed earlier, the church is comprised of diverse individuals as one body. The Holy Spirit brings us together in harmony through the goal of God's church: to follow His will, not our individual purposes.

Gordon Fee, in his book, *God's Empowering Presence*, explains it this way:

Forgiveness and Harmony

The church is Christ's Body. With this imagery, Paul essentially makes two main points in his letters about the church: the need for unity (harmony) and for diversity in the believing community, both of which are the work of "the one and the same Spirit."

First, the imagery of the church being Christ's body presupposes and contends for the unity of the people of God. That is the clear point of Ephesians 4. The church, composed of both Jew and Gentile, form one body. The urgency of the appeal for that begins in Ephesians 4:1 and carries through to the end is that they "Keep the unity that the Spirit has given them."

Second, the Holy Spirit is also responsible for maintaining a necessary and healthy diversity in the church. Every paragraph in 1 Corinthians 12 (except one) has this in them—the need for diversity in order for the community to be built up. God Himself as three Persons illustrates—and serves as the basis for—this diversity—in—unity. The Spirit who is responsible for their being one body is also the basis for the many parts necessary for the body to function at all. Significantly, the body imagery in Paul's letters with its concern for unity, focuses primarily on relationships within the church.

(Fee, G. D. (1994) *God's Empowering Presence.* Peabody, Mass: Hendrickson Publishers, Inc.)

APPLICATION

Bless those who persecute you; bless and do not curse. Rejoice with those who rejoice; mourn with those who mourn. Live in harmony with one another. Do not be proud, but be willing to associate with people of low position. Do not be conceited.

Romans 12:14-16

Make every effort to keep the unity of the Spirit through the bond of peace.

Ephesians 4:3

I want you to know how hard I am contending for you and for those at Laodicea, and for all who have not met me personally. My goal is that they may be encouraged in heart and united in love, so that they may have the full riches of complete understanding, in order that they may know the mystery of God, namely, Christ, in whom are hidden all the treasures of wisdom and knowledge.

Colossians 2:1-3

- How are the commands of forgiving others and living in harmony with others related?

- Are there people you purposely avoid when you see them?

    o   Why do you avoid them?

- After reading these scriptures, what will you do differently?

    <When> you stand praying, if you hold anything against anyone, forgive them, so that your Father in heaven may forgive you your sins.

Mark 11:25

Forgiveness and Harmony

When Joseph's brothers saw that their father was dead, they said, "What if Joseph bears a grudge against us and pays us back in full for all the wrong which we did to him!" ¹⁶ So they sent a message to Joseph, saying, "Your father charged before he died, saying, ¹⁷'Thus you shall say to Joseph, "Please forgive, I beg you, the transgression of your brothers and their sin, for they did you wrong."' And now, please forgive the transgression of the servants of the God of your father." And Joseph wept when they spoke to him. ¹⁸ Then his brothers also came and fell down before him and said, "Behold, we are your servants." ¹⁹But Joseph said to them, "Do not be afraid, for am I in God's place? ²⁰ As for you, you meant evil against me, but God meant it for good in order to bring about this present result, to preserve many people alive. ²¹ So therefore, do not be afraid; I will provide for you and your little ones." So he comforted them and spoke kindly to them.

Genesis 50:15-21 (NASB)

- How does living in unforgiveness damage our relationships with God and others?

- Are there any relationships with others in which you need to seek or offer forgiveness to repair the relationship?

  o How might you go about it?

- How did God use the sin of Joseph's brothers for His good purpose?

- Has God used a wrong committed against you for your good?

Live Love

- Who asked Joseph to forgive his brothers?

- Has anyone ever asked you to forgive someone else?

- Are you always obligated as a Christian to extend forgiveness?

For if you forgive other people when they sin against you, your heavenly Father will also forgive you. [15] But if you do not forgive others their sins, your Father will not forgive your sins.

Matthew 6:14-15

Therefore, as God's chosen people, holy and dearly loved, clothe yourselves with compassion, kindness, humility, gentleness and patience. [13] Bear with each other and forgive one another if any of you has a grievance against someone. Forgive as the Lord forgave you. [14] And over all these virtues put on love, which binds them all together in perfect unity.

Colossians 3:12-14

- Who has sinned against you recently?

  o Did you forgive them easily or did you hold onto the wrong they did to you?

- What does Jesus mean when He said if we do not forgive others, the Father will not forgive us?

  o What are the eternal ramifications of this?

- What should our attitude be as we seek forgiveness from others, according to Paul's words in Colossians?

- How would your life be different if you forgave those who hurt you?

- Can you think of someone with whom you have a grievance?

- How could you end the cycle of hurt this week?

- Have you forgiven yourself for your sin?

- Are there any past sins that creep up and bother you regularly?

- How would you rate yourself on a scale of 1-5 in the area of forgiving others and living in harmony with each other?

JOURNAL

Write down the names of those you need to forgive. Then list the reason(s) you think they hurt you. Finally, write down those from whom you need to seek forgiveness. As the Holy Spirit leads you in forgiving or seeking forgiveness, record the results. How did it feel to be forgiven? How did it feel to give forgiveness? What changed in your life? What would you do differently from this moment forward?

PRAYER

Heavenly Father I come to You because there is no way to repay the cost of my sin. It is impossible. Thank You for the cross and the blood of Your Son that covers all my sin. Thank You that based on that I can forgive the consequences of others' sins against me. Even though I can do this I need Your power to forgive as You forgave me. Holy Spirit please show me where my judgment is putting me in the place where only You belong. I am no one's judge but I need to be the forgiver of all as You are.

Father, I release others from my personal judgment and instead I choose to clothe myself in Your compassion. Let the compassion of the Lord Jesus who bled and died for me encompass me with kindness toward my brother or sister who has offended me. Lord Jesus, I want to love like You love, to be gentle as You are gentle, patient and humble as You walked in those graces as a pattern for us. I cannot do any of these things without Your power and without Your strength. Thank You that these things are abundant in You.

Live Love

NOTES

11

Obedience to God

¹³ Who is wise and understanding among you? Let them show it by their good life, by deeds done in the humility that comes from wisdom. ¹⁴ But if you harbor bitter envy and selfish ambition in your hearts, do not boast about it or deny the truth. ¹⁵ Such "wisdom" does not come down from heaven but is earthly, unspiritual, demonic. ¹⁶ For where you have envy and selfish ambition, there you find disorder and every evil practice.

¹⁷ But the wisdom that comes from heaven is first of all pure; then peace-loving, considerate, submissive, full of mercy and good fruit, impartial and sincere.¹⁸ Peacemakers who sow in peace reap a harvest of righteousness.

James 3:13-18

Obedience is the practice of obeying, as in submissive compliance. Verse 14 above shows a condition we are all susceptible to: *"if you have bitter jealousy and selfish ambition in your heart, do not be arrogant and lie against the truth."* Then verse 15 defines that attitude as earthly, unspiritual, and demonic. I believe the key to learning to obey and submit to God is to come clean and be honest about our rebellious heart. Once we admit that we have a rebellious nature, then we can start to deal with it.

Take This Job

About 27 years ago, I asked my mom why Dad quit working for Boise Cascade after 11 years. I don't know if she knew the exact answer but I remember her sharing this. I will never forget it.

"Your dad came home one day, told me he had quit, and said this to me: 'NO ONE WILL EVER TELL ME WHAT TO DO AGAIN AS LONG AS I LIVE.'"

That, my friends, is rebellion and a lack of submission. I believe God ordained that specific situation for Mom to share with me because I had a similar root of rebellion. I'm sure I had plenty of it on my own, but I felt the Holy Spirit tell me, in my early 20's, that I had to deal with a serious root of rebellion that was passed down from my dad.

My Story

Spring of 1989 was my last spring of college football at EWU. We were having a normal day in the weight room with 75-80 football players and coaches. Four of us were in our lifting routine as head coach Dick Zornes, "Coach Z," came up and asked how we were doing. As a senior, I was feeling spunky and said: "We're doing great, how about you Coach?"

About a second too late, I realized Coach Z wasn't in a good mood. Unfortunately, when he isn't in a good mood, you get the heck out of his way. Making matters worse, I'd been a Christian for two years, so I was supposed to be an example of Jesus, not the devil.

Coach Z mumbled a couple words and then filled the weight room with his sidelines voice. "Bradeen, are you doing your own thing here or are you following the prescribed lifting routine?"

Even though I was following the routine, I replied, "Coach, my routine is better."

Yep. Stupid. I know.

Coach Z grabbed my shirt and spoke straight through me. "Bradeen, you are a cocky bastard; you are a son of a b----- and you are *always* doing your own thing. Get the h--- out of my weight room!"

As I shuffled away, I realized that despite being a zealous Christian and loving Jesus, there were clearly rebellious issues in my life that needed to go. On the way to the shower, I heard the Holy Spirit speaking to me loudly, and I don't think I need to tell you what He was saying. Even though Coach Z was known for hating Christianity, I should have humbled myself as Jesus would have done and obeyed rather than shown my arrogance. Based on the scripture above from James, there was clearly demonic influence operating within me that needed some desperate attention.

Still, I will never be accused of being a quick learner. Nope. You can't put that on me.

In the summer of 1989, a few months after getting tossed from the weight room, I was in Yakima, WA, doing my two-week National Guard training. I'd been saved for two years, was on fire for God, and had no problem sharing my faith with those around me. I remember this training time especially well because I was the Tank Commander for the new 2nd Lieutenant. I recall we had multiple "God talks" during those two weeks. I'm sure I drove him completely nuts, but I felt I was doing my Christian duty by sharing Jesus.

Live Love

After six days of riding together in a tank, our unit had finished an offensive attack on another unit and was huddled together doing an after-actions report. About 20 minutes into the discussion, a small group of guys playing "the enemy" started firing down on us with machines guns. Even though the battle was officially over, they were still firing.

One of the sergeants and I decided we would have some fun and sneak up on them and fire back. So I grabbed the M60 machine gun, and the sergeant and I ran up a dry creek bed undetected. After 300 yards of sneaking up a ravine, we were 50 yards from them and still undetected. The sergeant gave the word and I lit up the small group of guys with all 100 practice rounds from my M60. When I was done, all had their lights and sirens going, meaning I'd killed them.

The sergeant and I were laughing and enjoying their shock when he said, "Okay, let's get back to camp the same way we came and sneak back down the creek bed."

Now, as a 21-year-old college football player and part-time Rambo who had just destroyed the enemy in a fake gun fight, I wasn't about to sneak back down the ravine. Instead, I argued with my sergeant—my military superior—telling him it was absolutely idiotic to sneak back down the ravine when we could just walk straight down the hill. Besides, I was the one carrying the M60.

Undeterred, he insisted we continue playing the military game and sneak back down to stay out of sight of the enemy. Well, being the humble, submissive Christian man that I wasn't, I told him to go to h---, then jumped out of the ravine and walked straight down the ridge to our camp. The sergeant, on the other hand, followed his own directive and sneaked back down the way we'd come.

About 45 minutes later, as I was sitting outside my tank

witnessing to the 2nd Lieutenant, I got a tap on the shoulder from our 1st Sergeant and was asked to come with him. He asked my opinion of the situation regarding the Sergeant and the order I'd ignored. Before I could finish talking, he began poking me in the chest and threatened me with an Article 15—a court martial—if I ever disobeyed a direct order again. This 1st Sergeant was a great man of character and highly respected. As he was finishing up my dressing down, the Holy Spirit convicted me so strongly that I repented to the 1st Sergeant immediately. I then went and did the same to the Sergeant and the 2nd Lieutenant. On the cusp of my triumphant war game ambush, I suddenly found my pride ambushed.

I was reminded of the conversation my mom had with me about my dad. His was not an attitude I wanted to live by. I realized I had an option to either obey the authority in my life or stay rebellious. Thankfully, I had the word of God that pierced my heart and mind, so I was able to repent of my rebellion and submit to God and the people around me.

After that two week training, I never saw the 2nd Lieutenant again and I don't remember our last conversation, but I'm certain it had an effect on his life, not because I told him about Jesus but because I came to him and repented of my pride. I'm sure he thought I was a crazy Christian with a big mouth, but after he saw me repent and apologize, I guarantee it became real and the Holy Spirit was able to convict his heart. If I had never repented to the authorities that I disobeyed, the 2nd Lieutenant would have had a good reason to bash Christians. Instead, he witnessed God in action.

Upon Further Review

During these two forays into abject stupidity that year, I did love Jesus and was obeying Him to the best of my ability. Clearly, there were fleshly pride and sin issues that needed to be dealt with, but I loved Jesus with all of my heart. In 1989, I had studied most of the scriptures I share in this book, so when I would sin and flex my disobedience muscle, the words would pop in my mind and help me deal with my issues.

Christians who sin by disobeying God and man's righteous authority don't concern Him as much as those who don't repent from the heart. God hates hypocrisy. Every person who followed Jesus during His brief earthly ministry sinned and disobeyed Him many times over. But the reason 120 believers obeyed Jesus and waited in Jerusalem for the outpouring of the Holy Spirit (Acts 2) is that they continually dealt with their sin through repentance and the pursuit of Jesus with all their heart.

We all have the same option. We can continue sinning and refuse to deal with our sin, reaping the wages of that sin and wondering why life is so difficult. Or we can deal with our sin, confront it with the perfect word of God, walk in accountability with the Holy Spirit and fellow believers, and grow to be like Jesus.

Obviously, Jesus came to save us and make us followers of Him. As we continue to follow Jesus, the Holy Spirit and the word of God will foster Jesus within us.

APPLICATION

Here is a quote from John G Lake in the early 1900s concerning God's will in the area of salvation of souls. It still rings true today. Above all, God has called us to win souls and bring them to maturity in Christ. Obedience to this call is the ultimate demonstration of our love for God.

Brother, Sister, when we stand before the bar of God

and are asked why we have not fulfilled in our life all the mind of Christ and all His desire in the salvation of the world, what will be our excuses if they are weighed against the salvation of imperishable souls. How terrible it will be for us to say we neglected, we put off, or we failed to seek for the endowment that comes from on high, the Baptism of the Holy Ghost.

Here is a great quote from Penn Jillette (from You Tube) who is a famous magician and also claims to be an atheist. It comes from someone who hates Christianity.

I've always said that I don't respect people who don't proselytize. I don't respect that at all. If you believe that there's a heaven and a hell, and people could be going to hell or not getting eternal life or whatever, and you think that it's not really worth telling them this because it would make it socially awkward—and atheists who think people shouldn't proselytize and who say just leave me along and keep your religion to yourself—how much do you have to hate somebody to not proselytize? How much do you have to hate somebody to believe that everlasting life is possible and not tell them that?

Penn Jillette

You Tube (2016, September 21)

Penn is telling Christians that if they actually believe what they teach, they should live by trying to convince others that Jesus is the Messiah. To me, he is basically telling Christians to obey Jesus. We should heed his words.

133

SELF EXAMINATION OR GROUP STUDY QUESTIONS

- Write down a list of non-believers that you are in weekly contact with. What are some ways that you can share Jesus with them?

- How is sharing the gospel ultimately the most loving thing you can do for another person?

- List some things that keep us from sharing the gospel?

- When it comes to biblical commands like obedience, loving God, and loving others, how would you rate yourself?

- How would you rate yourself in the area of sharing the salvation of Jesus with others?

As Jesus was walking beside the Sea of Galilee, he saw two brothers, Simon called Peter and his brother Andrew. They were casting a net into the lake, for they were fishermen. [19] "Come, follow me," Jesus said, "and I will make you fishers of men." [20] At once they left their nets and followed him.

Matthew 4:18-20

Then the eleven disciples went to Galilee, to the mountain where Jesus had told them to go. [17] When they saw him, they worshiped him; but some doubted. [18] Then Jesus came to them and said, "All authority in heaven and on earth has been given to me. [19] Therefore go and make disciples of all nations, baptizing them in the name of the Father and of the Son and of the Holy Spirit, [20] and teaching them to obey everything I have commanded you. And surely I am with you always, to the very end of the age."

Matthew 28:16-20

- What do you think Jesus meant by *I will make you fishers of men*?

- From all the scriptures in this book, how has God changed your thoughts, beliefs, and actions as you follow Jesus?

- Is making disciples an optional command?

- Considering these two scriptures, is your life more focused on your will and improving your life? Or is it more focused on doing God's will and making disciples?

We know that we have come to know him if we keep his commands. ⁴ Whoever says, "I know him," but does not do what he commands is a liar, and the truth is not in that person. ⁵ But if anyone obeys his word, love for God is truly made complete in them. This is how we know we are in him: ⁶ Whoever claims to live in him must live as Jesus did. Dear friends, I am not writing you a new command but an old one, which you have had since the beginning. This old command is the message you have heard. ⁸ Yet I am writing you a new command; its truth is seen in him and in you, because the darkness is passing and the true light is already shining.

⁹ Anyone who claims to be in the light but hates a brother or sister is still in the darkness. ¹⁰ Anyone who loves their brother and sister lives in the light, and there is nothing in them to make them stumble. ¹¹ But anyone who hates a brother or sister is in the darkness and walks around in the darkness. They do not know where they are going, because the darkness has blinded them.

1 John 2:3-11

Live Love

Do not love the world or anything in the world. If anyone loves the world, love for the Father is not in them. ¹⁶ *For everything in the world—the lust of the flesh, the lust of the eyes, and the pride of life—comes not from the Father but from the world.* ¹⁷ *The world and its desires pass away, but whoever does the will of God lives forever.*

1 John 2:15-17

- How would you define the phrase "complete obedience to Christ?"

- Why is obedience the ultimate form of love?

- Based on verses 15-17, would you say your life represents the world's system or God's system? Explain.

When they had finished eating, Jesus said to Simon Peter, "Simon son of John, do you love me more than these?" "Yes, Lord," he said, "you know that I love you." Jesus said, "Feed my lambs." ¹⁶ *Again Jesus said, "Simon son of John, do you love me?" He answered, "Yes, Lord, you know that I love you." Jesus said, "Take care of my sheep."* ¹⁷ *The third time he said to him, "Simon son of John, do you love me?" Peter was hurt because Jesus asked him the third time, "Do you love me?" He said, "Lord, you know all things; you know that I love you." Jesus said, "Feed my sheep.* ¹⁸ *Very truly I tell you, when you were younger you dressed yourself and went where you wanted; but when you are old you will stretch out your hands, and someone else will dress you and lead you where you do not want to go."* ¹⁹ *Jesus said this*

Obedience to God

to indicate the kind of death by which Peter would glorify God. Then he said to him, "Follow me!"

John 21:15-19

JOURNAL

I highly recommend writing down these commands from each chapter and spending quality time with Jesus, the Holy Spirit, and the Father. Let them shower you with their love, grace, and mercy. Jesus wants to take all our sin—our pain, offenses, unforgiveness, hatred, bitterness, selfish ambition, and insecurities. In its place, He wants to give us the power to walk in His love so we can teach others to do the same.

TWO PRAYERS

Van's prayer: Lord, I pray for these, my readers, to understand not just what is said here, but the spirit of what is imparted here. That they would come to see the unfathomable love of Jesus' great sacrifice—the gift of the Father to a people in great need. God, I seek the maturity of believers, that we emerge from Your incubator and launch lives intent on realizing a harvest for You—the reaping of mature souls for Your kingdom. May they become a people who know heaven on earth and the true nature of Your love. Amen.

Personal prayer: Father as I look at my life, I am seeing times that I acted on my own instead of obeying. I find better ways of doing things instead of going the way of faith and obedience. Thank You for forgiving me for disobeying, but I want to have a life of obeying You. I want to have a life that is a picture of You being my Lord. In that place of submitting to You, I want to live a life full of love, forgiveness, and dedication to You and to Your graces.

Because of acting in obedience to You, I pray that others would see You and Your power. I pray that the gospel would be seen in my life of obeying You so that others would ask about what they see in me. I then pray for the boldness to share Your great sacrifice of love for the world. Amen

NOTES

Conclusion

Repent! For the end of all things is near!!

Just kidding. It's just the end of the book.

With these final words, and as I've said many times throughout our study, I want to encourage and build you up. I want to show you that Jesus is for you. He has paved a way for you to commune with God every day, whether you are going through the storms of life or having the best day ever. Jesus is asking you to draw near to Him so He can heal you of all spiritual, emotional, and physical infirmities. Jesus *is* the author of *Live Love*!

CINDY DOCKINS

If you desire to see the proof of how God's word can heal and transform your life, read this amazing story from Cindy Dockins. Cindy and her husband Brian are elders in a great church in Old Town, ID, called House of the Lord.

Here is Cindy's testimony.

> Nothing extraordinary about that overcast March day. The extraordinary thing was the twinge of joy I felt in my heart.

> Two weeks earlier, I had written my goodbyes to my husband and each of our three children. I had no hope

and I was convinced God had forgotten me. Clinical depression for over a decade had finally won. I was done. After the notes were written, I spotted a cassette tape...The Prayer of Jabez for Women. Out of nothing better to do, I snapped it into my Walkman and clicked it on. And I listened and I listened. I listened every waking hour.

So it was on this day, March 4, 2007, fourteen years into my depression, that the Lord began to heal my mind. My healing confounded the medical profession, my friends and most of my family. My testimony of healing through scripture cannot be disputed or minimized, even by the biggest skeptics. My mind renewal has healed my marriage, my relationship with my children and now qualifies me to offer hope to the hopeless. God could have healed me miraculously, but He had a plan and a purpose. A plan to prosper not to harm.

Cindy Dockins

Cindy is someone who the world sees going through the storms of life, who then presses into God's word, and through the power of the Holy Spirit, they begin to transform into one who thinks, speaks, and acts like Jesus. Years ago, Cindy was on the couch ready to take her life, but today she is Living Love by ministering to ladies who need to be loved, healed, and set free from life's addictions. In addition, Cindy runs a ministry called New Song Ladies Ministry. It is based on Psalms 40:1-3.

I waited patiently for the Lord;
he turned to me and heard my cry.

Conclusion

He lifted me out of the slimy pit,
out of the mud and mire;
he set my feet on a rock
and gave me a firm place to stand.
He put a new song in my mouth,
a hymn of praise to our God.
Many will see and fear the Lord
and put their trust in him.

Psalm 40:1-3

As a Pastor/Shepherd, I am excited to see people come to Christ and then watch the Holy Spirit take new baby Christians and turn them into mature followers of Him—people who have hearts to see the wondrous work repeated in other lives. Everything I wrote in this book is possible to achieve through the power of the Holy Spirit in your life. Romans says: *faith comes from hearing the message, and the message is heard through the word about Christ* (Romans 10:17). One of my goals in writing this book is that you consume yourself with the word of God in each chapter, and by doing so, your faith in and relationship with Jesus vastly increases.

The book is ending, but your relationship with Jesus should be taking off to new heights of healing and excitement. The Apostle Paul was a radical person that wrote radical things about all the followers of Jesus having the ability to walk with Jesus and commune with the Holy Spirit every day to new levels of intimacy. When Jesus died and rose from the dead, He completely wiped your sin and shame away and gave you complete access to the Father.

Therefore, since we have been justified through faith, we have peace with God through our Lord Jesus Christ, through whom we have gained access by faith into this grace in which we now stand. And we boast in the hope of the glory of God.

Romans 5:1-2

He came and preached peace to you who were far away and peace to those who were near. ¹⁸ For through him we both have access to the Father by one Spirit. Consequently, you are no longer foreigners and strangers, but fellow citizens with God's people and also members of his household, ²⁰ built on the foundation of the apostles and prophets, with Christ Jesus himself as the chief cornerstone.

Ephesians 2:17-20

As you read these scriptures, know that you have been given access to God the Father through faith in Jesus Christ. The maker of heaven and the entire universe has opened His door to you so you can come and dwell in His presence. It seems like so much of the Christian life is spent working our way to God and trying to convince ourselves that we might be good enough to someday to be in the presence of the Father. The enemy of our soul loves to keep us in this thought process of earning our way to God; he speaks condemnation over us and accuses us of our sin all day long. But the writers of the New Testament tell us that we have been given access to God for all of our healing so we can walk in wholeness and live love. The enemy says, "You are not good enough to open that door," but God's word says that Jesus hung on the cross so we might be forgiven of all of our sins, giving us an open door to the Father.

As you devour God's word and allow it to transform you into a Live Love Human Being, the love of God will consume you. Paul wrote that God wants each of us to experience God's presence and love in ways far beyond our imaginations.

Let us let God have the last word in our studies. Remember, these scriptures were written for *you.*

> *For this reason, ever since I heard about your faith in the Lord Jesus and your love for all God's people, ¹⁶ I have not stopped giving thanks for you, remembering you in my prayers. ¹⁷ I keep asking that the God of our Lord Jesus Christ, the glorious Father, may give you the Spirit of wisdom and revelation, so that you may know him better. ¹⁸ I pray that the eyes of your heart may be enlightened in order that you may know the hope to which he has called you, the riches of his glorious inheritance in his holy people, ¹⁹ and his incomparably great power for us who believe. That power is the same as the mighty strength ²⁰ he exerted when he raised Christ from the dead and seated him at his right hand in the heavenly realms, ²¹ far above all rule and authority, power and dominion, and every name that is invoked, not only in the present age but also in the one to come.*

> Ephesians 1:15-21

> *But because of his great love for us, God, who is rich in mercy, ⁵ made us alive with Christ even when we were dead in transgressions—it is by grace you have been saved. ⁶ And God raised us up with Christ and seated us with him in the heavenly realms in Christ Jesus, ⁷ in order that in the coming ages he might show the incomparable riches of his grace, expressed in his kindness to us in Christ Jesus. ⁸ For it is by*

grace you have been saved, through faith—and this is not from yourselves, it is the gift of God— [9] not by works, so that no one can boast. [10] For we are God's handiwork, created in Christ Jesus to do good works, which God prepared in advance for us to do.

Ephesians 2:4-10

I pray that out of his glorious riches he may strengthen you with power through his Spirit in your inner being, [17] so that Christ may dwell in your hearts through faith. And I pray that you, being rooted and established in love, [18] may have power, together with all the Lord's holy people, to grasp how wide and long and high and deep is the love of Christ, [19] and to know this love that surpasses knowledge—that you may be filled to the measure of all the fullness of God.

Ephesians 3:16-19

About The Author

Van Bradeen was raised in Inchelium, WA, on the Colville Indian Reservation. He grew up exploring mountains, hunting, fishing, and playing high school football. God first reached his heart in the eighth grade during a four-day Bible camp. He was profoundly affected during this time but soon reverted to being (in his words) a "knucklehead." In 1987, while Van was playing football for Eastern Washington University, Jesus entered his dorm room and began a radical transformation that endures to this day. Soon afterward, God gave him a vision for shepherding God's people.

Through the mentoring of many good people, Van grew into the role to which he was called. Today, Van and his wife Lori are lead pastors of Living Stone Church, in Spokane, WA, a church they pioneered. They have three children, all serving the Lord.

Van's passion is to see people come to a living knowledge of the love of God, walking as disciples of His word, led by His Spirit, and following His son.

For further information, or to contact Van, use this email: VanBradeen@gmail.com.

Made in the USA
San Bernardino, CA
11 August 2017